Bill Borden

Bill Borden

by

Dick Bohrer

MOODY PRESS

CHICAGO

Library of Congress Cataloging in Publication Data

Bohrer, Dick.
Bill Borden.

Summary: Presents the life of the Christian missionary as recalled by his friends and associates.
1. Borden, William. 2. Missionaries—United States—Biography. 3. Missions to Muslims—History—19th century.
4. Missions to Muslims—History—20th century.
[1. Borden, William. 2. Missionaries] I. Title.
BV2626.B67B64 1984 280'.4 [B] [92] 84-10792
ISBN 0-8024-0390-5

1 2 3 4 5 6 7 Printing DP Year 89 88 87 86 85 84

Printed in the United States of America

Contents

Introduction

Perhaps the one person God used most in the formation of Bill Borden's life—and in its transformation to likeness to Christ—was his mother. He learned to love and worship God at her knee. He learned his reverence for God's Word from her. He was sensitive to spiritual concerns because she was sensitive.

He was born to wealth, but she kept that matter-of-fact in his life. He was born under authority, and she taught him to respect it. He was healthy and mischievous, so she taught him self-restraint. She bred in him a love of learning and a love for having fun. Her love touched his spirit and turned him heavenward. When her time came to let him go, she did so willingly, knowing whose hands would take hold.

Her own experience with Christ took on new meaning when William was seven. She became an earnest, rejoicing Christian in a way she had never known. Living along Chicago's "Gold Coast" of lovely homes, she found it convenient to transfer her church membership to nearby Moody Church where Dr. R. A. Torrey was pastor. There William both received Christ as his Savior and took his first tentative steps toward dedicating his life to His service.

Mrs. Borden taught William to love God's Word, and she spent time with him daily in prayer. They would pray before he left for school that he "might know in his experience the power of the blood of Jesus Christ." As he grew older, they prayed that the will of God would be done in his life.

Bill attended the University School and the Latin and Manual Training Schools in Chicago. He finished the last two years of high school at the Hill School, a private preparatory school for boys, in Pottstown, Pennsylvania.

A number of people watched William Whiting Borden during the last nine years of his life. Some knew him well—some very well. His story is their story; it's only right that they should tell it.

The narrative is based on their letters and on records of fact. Dialogue has been supplied. The author is indebted to Mrs. Howard Taylor whose book, *William Borden, A Life and Fortune Dedicated to the Cause of the Gospel,* formed the basis of this new work.

—Dick Bohrer

1

Walter Erdman

(Bill's adult companion on his world tour)

Bill never knew that summer of 1904 that he had only nine years left. Life was too exciting to even think of things like that.

Half of Chicago seemed to be swarming around us as we stood with his family on the platform of the railroad station.

"Make sure you always have a handkerchief, William," his mother said as she poked at the one in his breast pocket.

"And I expect you to obey Mr. Erdman implicitly. William. Are you listening?" His father's voice brought Bill's eyes back to reality. There was so much for him to see. Porters were ushering people on board, and baggage was being trundled on big wagons toward the baggage car. Passengers were calling their good-byes. We were just starting a trip that had been a long time in planning. Both of us were numb with excitement.

"I said, William, are you listening?"

"Oh, yes, Father," Bill said, "I'll do everything he says."

"Not just today, but all year long."

"Yes, Father."

The conductor was calling all aboard.

"And don't forget to bring me something," his sister Joyce said. "And something for Mary"—his sister at Vassar College.

"And write." His mother turned his face so that he would look at her. "You will write, won't you, William?"

He flung his arms around her. "Of course, I'll write."

I went up the steps. "We'd better get aboard."

Late passengers were running now. The train tooted twice and began to move.

"Just one more kiss," Bill said to his mother.

She gave him a quick peck, and he ran to catch the train, which had begun to accelerate. He caught the pole beside the stairs of the end car and swung himself up. He looked back with a grin and waved.

"William," his father called sharply. His voice carried over all the terminal noise. "Don't do things like that! It isn't fair to Mr. Erdman."

I watched the boy nod and wave again as the train moved out of the darkness of the terminal and into the sunshine of the summer day. He was excited about going, but I knew he'd really miss his mother.

"It's not every sixteen-year-old who gets to see the world," I said.

Bill kept waving until he knew his family couldn't see him anymore. "I'm surprised myself they let me go," he said. "What with Japan and Russia still fighting and us going to Yokohama and Tokyo on our first leg."

"Oh, I don't think there's any real danger," I said. "Come on inside and let's give this train the once-over. We're going to be living here three days, you know."

We became better acquainted in our stateroom. I

had just come out from New Jersey where I'd graduated from Princeton. I really didn't know Bill very well. His parents had contacted me through mutual friends because I knew his brother John, also a student at Yale.

We answered the first call for dinner.

"How did you do in school?" I asked him while we waited for our soup.

"Oh, not good, not bad. I had an 83.6 percent average there at the end."

"First in your class?"

"No, fourth. I really had to work hard. I had a lot of trouble with geometry and English Lit—ugh."

"Oh, I liked English Lit—Milton, Keats—"

"Not me. I joined the gun club and was second string on the football team. It was a wonderful school. I'll never forget the friends I made there."

"Gun club. Football team. You don't sound like the kind that—you know—likes to sit around and talk or go to museums and look at antiques."

"Not me," Bill shook his head. "I've got to keep moving."

The waiter brought the soup.

"Tell me about John Meigs, your headmaster," I said.

"Oh, he was a real man. Um, this is good soup."

"A real man? What do you mean?"

"He knew what being a man is all about. He always said the strength of manhood is built on purity and that impurity is weakness and shame. I can hear him now." Bill sat up straight and spoke low. "Self-reverence, self-knowledge, self-control lead life to sovereign power."

We laughed. "Those are good words," I said.

"Oh, he meant them all right. And you know

what else he used to say?"

"What?"

"He told us the test of our religious life is what we are and what we do when we're not on our knees in prayer, when we're not reading our Bible or listening to great preachers or going to religious meetings."

"He's a wise man."

The waiter cleared the dishes and brought our salads.

"He said he wanted us to choose the Lord Jesus as the pattern for our lives."

"And what do you say?"

Bill looked out the window and then looked me in the eye. "I really do want the Lord to be the pattern for my life."

I reached over and slapped him on the arm. "We're going to get along fine, Bill," I said. "I want the very same thing. And if we can live like that for the whole year we'll be traveling together, we'll really have a good time. The Lord will see to that."

Bill pointed down the car. "See those two men over there? They prayed before they started to eat. Why don't we ask them to join us?"

I turned and saw two young men my age—probably seminary graduates too—laughing and talking over their soup. "Good idea," I said. I rose to go meet them.

When we got on board the USS *Korea* in San Francisco, Bill wrote his mother. He let me read the letter.

> We're off at last, and so far it seems quite nice, although in some respects a little speck disappointing.

We went down to the wharf quite early and our bags were taken up to the room by a lot of little Chinamen dressed in dark blue with a round black hat with a red top-knot to it. They were certainly very funny and cute. Most of them take the end of their queue and put it in their coat pocket. Our steward is a very nice Chinaman dressed like the ones I have just described.

The scene at the dock was quite queer, very different from the departure of an Atlantic steamer. Chinamen swarmed everywhere, and there were also a good many Japanese mixed in. All the servants and sailors are Chinamen and they seem to be very competent. Some of them are comical in their appearance and actions and I enjoy watching them, especially the sailors going about their work.

Our fellow passengers are mostly married people; in fact, there aren't more than half a dozen young folk that I have noticed. The Chinamen are by far the most interesting bunch.

Bill was intrigued with the way the Chinese ate with chopsticks. The next day he wrote his mother again:

Today we have gotten pretty well settled and have had a chance to look around a bit. Our chairs are located on the port side, near the forward end of the promenade deck. Our neighbors are a couple of young men starting out as missionaries. They are Jones and Gibb and were on the train with us coming out to San Francisco.

Then there is a Mr. Lamb and his wife and little boy. Mr. Lamb is a classmate of Walter's, and he and his wife are going to the Philippines as missionaries. They are very nice and awfully jolly.

Bill and my friend Lamb got permission to tour

the ship, and Bill wrote his mother all about the men in the boiler room. He had an eye for detail and always seemed conscious of his surroundings.

> The color of the water out here as it surges away from the ship is remarkable. It is a deep indigo blue and doesn't seem to be affected by the color of the sky.

Our ship stopped a day in Honolulu to pick up more passengers and cargo. Native boys, hoping the passengers would toss them coins to dive for, swam out to meet the ship. Some scrambled on board and dove from the lifeboats. Bill and I went swimming and surfing, took in the aquarium, and drove to points of interest on the island.

On October 4, he wrote his Uncle Fred and Aunt Laura:

> Going round the world may be quite a trip, but it isn't anything uncommon among these passengers. There are three or four who are on their fourth trip around, and several on their third or second. So we sink into insignificance. We have a couple of German and Austrian Counts and Countesses, an Italian doctor and also several German university men, one with scars on his cheek. Then there is an Admiral of the U.S. Navy and a Bishop. So you see we have quite a few celebrities.
>
> We have only seen the smoke of one boat since we left San Francisco. The Pacific is quite large.

Yokohama introduced us to the new Japan. Thousands of years of Far East tradition were finally merging with modernization from the West. I was struck by the buildings, but Bill couldn't take his eyes off the people. Children were everywhere, dressed in bright kimonos. He wrote his sister Joyce: "They all wear queer little wooden clogs which they hold on with the big toe and the next one."

We made a point of visiting the Buddhist temples. One we went to was on top of a hill overlooking the sea. It was the temple of the goddess of mercy, and it contained a number of idols on shelves around the walls. One was cluttered with pieces of paper. We learned that these were prayers. A worshiper pulls a piece of paper off a string hanging nearby, chews it a while, and throws it at the idol. If it sticks, the prayers are answered—otherwise, not.

In Tokyo we were permitted to drive through the palace grounds of the Mikado and visit the Houses of Parliament.

Bill wrote his mother:

> The room in which the Representatives meet is simple and not unusual. The House of Peers is much more gorgeous—especially the Mikado's office-room. This is beautifully fitted out with gold-lacquer screens and a cloth of gold over the desk. The Imperial box also is very fine with such things as silks and gold lace.

After our climb up Mt. Fuji, he wrote her:

> We had a hot sulphur bath which was simply great! The Japanese tubs are made of wood and are about three feet deep and oblong in shape. Instead of climbing into them you step down. I think they are fine and enjoy boiling in them up to my neck! I am afraid they will spoil me for any others.

In Kyoto he was impressed by another Buddhist temple. He wrote:

> The most interesting temple we visited was the

Sangusanguido or Temple of the 33,333 gods. The building that contains this outfit is a shabby-looking place about four hundred feet long by sixty wide. The images all represent the same goddess, Kivanna, goddess of mercy. They are made of wood and gilded.

Right opposite the entrance is a huge image said to be carved out of one willow tree. On either side are five hundred idols, each about five feet high. They are arranged in ten rows of fifty, each row rising above the one in front of it. The images are meant to represent the eleven-faced-thousand-handed goddess of mercy, but they only have one face and twenty-one pairs of hands. I suppose it would have been too much work to make them all. The 33,333 are obtained by counting the small effigies held in the hands and in the halos of the large ones. It is a very strange sight.

On November 1 I gave him a letter.

"From Mom?"

"Sure is."

"She knew how to time it. Right to the day. I wonder how she figured out how to get it here the exact day."

"She didn't."

"Oh?"

"No, I've had it. She wrote me that she wanted me to intercept it and keep it until your birthday."

"Scoundrel!"

"Well, open it and read it."

Bill unsealed it and drew out two sheets, neatly folded.

I waited while he read. "Any news?"

"No. Just wishing me a happy seventeenth. And she asks me to pray to God for His very best plan for my life."

"What's the other sheet?"
"Looks like a poem."
"Read it."
He read:

Just as I am, Thine own to be,
Friend of the young, who lovest me,
To consecrate myself to Thee—
O Jesus Christ, I come.
In the glad morning of my day,
My life to give, my vows to pay,
With no reserve and no delay—
With all my heart, I come.
I would live ever in the light,
I would work ever for the right,
I would serve Thee with all my might—
Therefore to Thee I come.
Just as I am, young, strong and free,
To be the best that I can be
For truth and righteousness and Thee—
Lord of my life, I come.

Bill sat, saying nothing. I quietly left. I learned much later that he kept that poem near him the rest of his life. It went with him to Yale and to Princeton. It was among his personal papers at the end.

2

Walter Erdman (Cont.)

Bill shook the rail when I told him. "A girl? An American girl?"

"That's right," I said. "When we get to Nanking, we'll be staying with the Stewarts." We were standing on deck of a steamer taking us up the wide Yangtze River to Hankow.

"I haven't seen an American girl in—how many months have we been away?"

I laughed again. "We've been gone seven weeks and all you can think of is girls. If your folks knew this, they'd have kept you home."

"But that's the trouble with traveling." Bill ran his hands through his hair. "Oh, it's great to see the world, but you have to do it with old people. Why aren't people my age traveling around?"

"Well, thanks a lot!"

"Oh, I didn't mean you, Walt. It's just that I miss people my age."

He wrote his mother:

> I have come to the conclusion that young people of either sex never travel out here and in fact don't exist! I almost feel as though we were breaking the rules.

> We have met scarcely any young people. There were two fellows and two or three girls on our ship out, no more. In Japan, none. However, we hope for better things as we reach more civilized regions.

Seeing the Stewart girl did a lot to assure him that real American girls can and do live in Asia.

After seeing Hankow and Nanking, we went to Canton. You can't believe it until you see it. There are 350,000 boat people living in small sampans along the river bank. They line up ten deep and they choke all the small canals. One boat is about twenty feet long and a family of six or seven will live their entire life on the water. They keep chickens in cages hung out over the water. Women and children wear an empty can at their back in case they should fall overboard.

We learned that one Chinese will seldom rescue another because the rescuer has to keep the rescued for the rest of his life, if he happens to want to be kept. Sometimes they will bargain with a drowning man before pulling him out. But the river people live and die on their boats. The land people won't let them on shore. They don't want their businesses taken away from them.

When we visited the Young Men's Christian Association chapter in Canton, Bill got involved witnessing. He talked to a young businessman who said he was a Christian and made much of the fact that he always went to church. But he began railing at missions and saying they were no good. Bill tried to defend them but found, as the conversation deepened, that the man was practically an infidel and didn't believe anything the Bible said.

Bill told him what he believed. The man said Bill

was young and didn't know any better. In a few years he would think differently.

The incident was good for Bill. It made him realize just how much he knew—or didn't know—his Bible.

Bill caught typhoid in Canton, and the doctors put him to bed. It meant we would have to cancel Java and limit the amount of time we'd have for India. But it was interesting to watch Bill when he was confined to a bed and couldn't do the moving about he preferred.

His Bible was always on his bed in the hospital, except when the fever was at its height. I remember finding him poring over the tenth chapter of Genesis one morning with a new interest in its geographical and ethnological statements, aroused by his first impressions of new races and men of other tongues. It was a little Bible with fine print, too fine indeed for practical use. But it must have become dear to him for I have seen it since, open on his study table at Princeton.

You'd think the milestones in our trip were the girls we met, to listen to Bill. It was June, and we had concluded our trip to China, visited Hong Kong and the Straights Settlements, India, Egypt, Palestine, and Asia Minor, and finally the chief cities of Greece and Italy. In Venice, we'd been invited to join an American woman and her daughter on a moonlight ride in their gondola.

"She's a girl, isn't she?"

"Yes, Bill," I told him, "she's a girl. But she's too old for you."

"No girl is too old for me when I haven't seen one for half way around the world. How old is she?"

"All I know is she's the lady's daughter."

"Do you realize we have met only three American girls on our whole trip? Three, Walt. Three."

"She's a graduate of Bryn Mawr, and she's under appointment as a missionary to India."

"Wonderful. But does she know what India's like?"

"I suppose so."

"Well, we'll have to tell her. Maybe Venice won't be so bad after all."

We enjoyed being poled up and down the Grand Canal. Then we lay alongside one of the singing barges and listened to the music for an hour or so.

"You had how long in India?" the daughter asked. "Tell me about it."

"Not quite two months," Bill said. "We really covered the continent. We took trips to the foothills of the Himalayas, hunting expeditions in the central provinces—"

"What did you hunt?"

"They called it the spiral-horned black buck. I got one, too."

"What else did you see?"

"Oh, we went to the Taj Mahal and the temples of South India. Wait'll you see them—or maybe you shouldn't. Yeah, I don't think you should go to them, should she, Walt?"

"I'm not a child," she said. "What were they like?"

"Well—"Bill seemed hesitant. "Well, inside the temples they have a lot of images and corridors with wonderful stone monoliths. In the center of the temple in Madura is a pool called the Tank of the Golden Lilies—but I don't know why they call it that. The water was covered with green slime. I couldn't figure out why the people would wash themselves and their clothes in it. They were even drinking it."

"It's supposed to wash away their sins," I interrupted.

"Of course, we weren't allowed to go into some of the inner chambers, and I guess it was just as well. We were told the worship of Siva—that's what this temple is given over to—is about the foulest thing you can imagine."

"Don't they worship several gods?" she asked.

"Well, the three principal Hindu gods are—Walt, help me—Brahma—"

"He's the creator god," I said.

"And Vishnu—"

"The preserver."

"And Siva—"

"The destroyer and the reproducer."

"Yeah, Hinduism is awful. You can't imagine how vile it is. Hinduism hasn't done anything for those people. You wonder why they worship like that."

"It's a degrading worship," I said. "They worship lust and vice. Tens of thousands of women and children are caught up in prostitution in the temples."

Our hostess raised an eyebrow and looked at her daughter.

"What impressed you the most, Bill?" the girl asked.

"Two things, I guess—two of the most unforgettable. The Himalayas, for one. We got up to seven thousand feet in Darjeeling, and then we took a horseback ride up to nine thousand feet on Tiger Hill. We nearly froze. But we got there just at dawn, and the effects of light and shade were wonderful. On our right we had a perfect wall of snow-capped peaks about twenty thousand feet high, stretching off for a hundred miles. Directly west was the range with Kichenjunga in it. Then more to the left was a line of foothills about twelve thousand feet high, wooded and without snow. Beyond these, when the sun got higher, we could see the peak of Everest, 120 miles away. With our glasses, we could see the sharp lines and the great bare cliffs near the top." Bill sighed. "It was marvelous."

"I can't wait," she said. "And what was the second thing?"

"Benares."

"Benares? The city?"

"Not so much the city as the Ganges River. The city is considered so holy that people think if they die there they'll have eternal happiness for sure. Lots of pilgrims come there simply to die."

"How gruesome."

"And the Ganges! The people are bathing in it all the time. They wash themselves and their clothes in it, pray to it, drink it, and throw their dead in it. You'll need to rent a boat when you get there. You get a much better view from the river. We did this twice."

"I don't know that I want to."

"You should! The weather is so strange. I shivered all day—it was so cold. And then we read in the paper that night that in the sun the temperature had been 120 degrees."

"What else did you see?"

"The burning ghats."

"The what?"

"They put a corpse on a funeral pyre in the river and they burn it. When it is ashes, they throw it into the river—with people bathing not fifty feet away."

"India's millions," I said, "are doing their best to wash their sins away, not realizing that Christ has already done it."

Bill saw that, and it marked him for life. He wrote his mother:

> Walt and I have Bible study together every day when possible, and I enjoy it very much. He is able to point out many things that are new to me, and I am beginning to see what a wonderful storehouse of good things the Bible is. I pray every day for all my dear family. I also pray that God will take my life into His hands and use it for the furtherance of His Kingdom as He sees best. I feel sure that He will answer my prayer. It strengthens me to know that you are also praying for this.
>
> I have so much of everything in this life, and there are so many millions who have nothing and live in darkness! I don't think it is possible to realize it until one sees the East. I know it is no *easy* thing to serve the Lord; but others have been enabled to do so, and there is no reason why I should not. Mark 10:27.

He also wrote her two letters in May and June, 1905, that reveal how deeply rooted his new conviction had become.

> I am glad that you have told Father about my desire to be a missionary. I am thinking about it all the time and looking forward to it with a good deal of anticipation. I know that I am not at all fitted or prepared yet, but in the next four or five years I ought to be able to prepare myself. I have been reading Mr. Speer's book on Missionary Principles and Practice. It is very good, in my opinion. He takes up the different kinds of missionary work—educational, medical and evangelistic—and discusses them with regard to the different countries. You may have read it, and if you haven't I think you would like it.
>
> I don't think I want to go through a Seminary, but thorough Bible study is what I do need. As Dr.

Torrey says, "It's much more important and profitable to know what God has to say on a subject than what men have to say." I would like some medical skill . . . enough so as not to be absolutely helpless and ignorant. But I really oughtn't to try and form plans of my own but let God do it for me, and then it's sure to be right . . . I will be mighty glad when I can talk things over with you.

And about three weeks later, he wrote:

I have just finished reading Mr. Speer's book. It has helped me a great deal. I especially noticed the two chapters he takes to the Student Volunteer Movement. He shows very clearly what the motto, "The Evangelization of the World in this Generation" means, and how perfectly possible it is, provided we pray the Lord of the harvest to send forth laborers. There is something inspiring in the project to me. It is something fine, something worth every effort to accomplish and which will repay us when we have done our duty.

When I got through reading, I knelt right down and prayed more earnestly than I have for some time for the mission work and for God's plan for my life, and also for His plans for the lives of every one of my family. Oh, Mother, do pray for me. College is so near and there will be such a lot of things to do, tremendous opportunities! Pray that I may be guided in everything, small and great.

The highlight of our visit to Switzerland was the opportunity Bill and I had to do some mountain climbing in the Alps. Our first mountain was the Titlis, eleven thousand feet high. We left Lucerne by train for Engelberg. Hiring a good guide and renting hiking equipment, we set out for Trubsee, an hour and a half away. Looking down from the window of a little hotel perched on the edge of a cliff, we could see the town and valley of Engelberg. Here we had our first glass of fresh milk since leaving America.

Behind the hotel rose a range of snow-covered mountains, the Titlis among them. We started our walk about half past two the next morning and, moving slowly but steadily, climbed for nearly an hour and a half. After a short rest, we tackled the major part of the ascent. We arrived about sunup and reveled in the view of Interlaken, Monte Rosa, the Dome, and Jungfrau. Bill never got over his love for mountain climbing after that hike. He had a strong physique and enjoyed the rigors of the trail.

But he breathed an obvious sigh of relief when we reached Britain. "What bliss to be back in a land where people talk English!" he wrote his mother.

There wasn't a sporting event he and I didn't take in. We saw tennis at Wimbledon, rowing on the Thames, and we watched the Cambridge-Oxford cricket match. We also saw all the major buildings in the city. But London gave him the most significant experience of his trip in quite another way.

Dr. R. A. Torrey had been holding meetings in London for five months. The first Sunday in July, Bill and I took in the afternoon meeting. Bill took careful notes. He wrote his mother:

> The text was John 3:6, "That which is born of the flesh is flesh, and that which is born of the Spirit is spirit"—and Dr. Torrey gave five proofs by which we can tell whether we are "born again," born of the Spirit, or not. Every proof was a verse of Scripture. That's what I like, lots of the Word of God and little of man.

This renewed contact with Dr. Torrey, his pastor at Moody Church, was the turning point of Bill's life. A conscientious student, a dutiful son, a relentless competitor, he had not really signed his name to full commitment to Christ until then.

The way he took notes shows how his logical mind moved. Torrey's five proofs were as follows:

1st. 1 John 2:29. *"Every one that doeth righteousness is born of Him."* Righteousness equals such actions as are straight. Straight action is conduct that is conformed to a straight edge. And the straight edge of life is the Word of God. Righteousness equals the practice of such actions as are conformed to the Word of God. Do we practice righteousness? If we do, we are born of God.

2nd. 1 John 3:9. *"Whatsoever is born of God doth not commit sin."* Sin is something done, a breaking of the law; and the law is the revealed will of God. Sin, therefore, is transgression of the will of God. "Every one that doeth sin, doeth also lawlessness: and sin is lawlessness." 1 John 3:4. The regenerate man does not wilfully and intentionally sin.

3rd. 1 John 3:14. *"We know that we have passed out of death into life because we love the brethren."* The brethren are all those who believe in the Lord Jesus Christ. Love for the brethren, positive and negative, is explained in verses 16-18. We ought to love to the extent of giving our lives—literally, if necessary—as God did for us. "Let us not love in word, neither with the tongue, but in deed and in truth," v. 18. Love for the brethren is a proof of rebirth.

4th. 1 John 5:1. *"Whosoever believeth that Jesus is the Christ is born of God."* Christ equals the Anointed One of God. Belief equals absolute conviction. Whosoever is convinced absolutely that Jesus is the Anointed One of God is born of God.

5th. 1 John 5:4. *"Whosoever is born of God overcometh the world."* A regenerate person has that within him which overcomes the world.

Summary: One who is "born again" practices righteousness; is not committing sin; loves the brethren; believes that Jesus is the Christ; overcomes the world. We cannot do all this by ourselves, therefore what are we to do? Answer, John 1:12. "As many as *received* Him, to them gave He power to become the sons of God, even to them that believe on His Name." So we have only to believe in Jesus and receive Him, and immediately we have power to become sons of God.

(The next thing to do is to use this power. W.W.B.)

In another meeting, an invitation was given to those who had never publicly indicated that they had surrendered all to Christ. Bill stood up with several others as the congregation sang:

> I surrender all, I surrender all;
> All to Thee, my blessed Savior,
> I surrender all.

Torrey spoke to those who stood, giving them five points for daily living:

1. Look always at Jesus.
2. Keep confessing Jesus everywhere.
3. Keep studying God's Word (Matthew 4:4).
4. Keep praying every day (1 Thessalonians 5:17).
5. Go to work.

Bill wrote his mother, "The first four I am doing and the fifth I will do."

When he got home from the service that night, he felt there was a difference. In days following, he found power to give up using some slang expressions that he felt were displeasing to the Lord. And, one night, "I prayed not only that my life might be controlled but my thoughts, also, and meant it. I expected a direct answer and got it the next day, and I have been kept in that matter ever since. I don't think I ever had any real definite experience like that before, and it strengthened my faith."

It also strengthened his interest in personal witnessing.

Walking to visit a friend one evening, he joined a street-corner gospel service. When the meeting was over, he stood witnessing to a young man who had read books written by a critic of the Word. Finally, the man gave Bill his address and said he'd like to talk to him further.

The next day, Bill bought A. T. Pierson's book *Many Infallible Proofs* and then spent the afternoon looking for his friend. The address proved phony.

Any disappointment he might have felt was displaced by the enjoyment he found from having freedom in witnessing to an unbeliever, something he had not experienced before, he told me.

I left Bill at Camden, at the summer home on the coast of Maine his father had recently built. I knew the golf links, the swimming, the yachting would really appeal to Bill; but by now I knew he would find deeper joy in the times he could be alone with his mother.

My own ministry eventually took me to Korea, but I will never forget the inspiration of his friendship and love and his loyalty to Christ. I learned more things from Bill about simplicity of faith and steadfastness of purpose than he did from me, and the memory of our comradeship will be dearly prized until we meet again.

3

Charlie Campbell

(Bill's close friend at Yale)

The first time I met Bill, a number of us were crowded together in Bill Barnes's room. Barnes, a Yale junior, was vice-president of the Young Men's Christian Association and leader of religious work among the college's freshmen. Borden was sitting on the floor with his back against the wall and his knees drawn up near his chin. I remember noticing him particularly. As we left the meeting he joined me—

"Where do you live?"

"Pierson," I said. It was the one college-owned dormitory on York Street and not considered as swell as the privately owned dorms. "You?"

"Oh, Garland's." He said it so matter-of-factly. You didn't live there unless your family had money.

"I hear you've just come back from a trip around the world."

"I've just come back from having my eyes opened. You wouldn't believe how people live in China and India and how spiritually blind they are. They throw spit wads at an idol and think that's how you get your prayers answered."

We talked about it as we walked and found we had

a lot in common. That was the beginning of our friendship, and it would last till Bill's dying day. I will admit, though, that my first impulse after seeing his room at Garland's was to be aloof. I felt sure he was too well-off to have much to do with me. I not only lived at Pierson, I lived on the fifth floor. Anyone coming to see me had to really want to see me. And Bill came—not once but often! And what times we would have. His love of fun was sure to show itself, and we'd often have a good roughhouse. One evening we staged a complete track meet in my room, and Bill was the man to beat in almost every event.

In the fall Bill went out for the freshman football team and really played good ball. He just missed making the team. In fact, in the game with the Princeton freshmen, he was told to warm up to go in. But they called time—or something like that—and forgot they needed him.

It was well into our first term when Bill and I began to pray together in the morning before breakfast. I don't remember whose suggestion it was, but I'm fairly sure Bill thought it up. We'd been meeting only a short time when Farrand Williams asked to join us, and soon after that, James Howard. We met in Bill's room and prayed after a brief reading of Scripture. Our object was to pray for the religious work of the class and college and also for those of our friends we were seeking to bring to Christ. Bill was a real stimulus in those meetings. He knew his Bible and he'd always show us something new and fresh, something God had promised. And in his prayer he would claim that promise with real assurance.

Our prayer group started with just us two, but by

the end of our sophomore year it had grown so large that it had to be divided. Similar groups were meeting in each of the classes. This was one movement that began with the freshmen and moved up to the seniors rather than the other way around. And the Lord really answered our prayers—a number of men were converted.

Bill had a lot of trouble with one guy who had a scientific turn of mind and wanted everything proved. Had Bill lived, he would have been thrilled when, some years later, this man came to Christ and began living for Him.

Borden was like that—always picking out the toughest proposition and going through thick and thin to win him to Christ.

Some of us tried to figure it out.

"What's his secret," someone said. "He's got the same temptations all of us have."

"Remember when Dr. John R. Mott spoke to us on the verse, 'Be sure your sin will find you out?'" I said. "He asked, when he finished, for all of us who wanted to learn how to deal with temptation to meet in another room. I went with him—and Bill was there."

"So what's his secret?"

I don't remember who, but somebody said, "He's just gotten a head start on the rest of us. When he got here he was ahead of all of us spiritually. He'd already given his heart in full surrender to Christ, and set his sights on being a missionary. He knows what he wants and he's out to get it."

And that was right. Bill had a settled purpose and determination that made him solid as a rock. Oh, I'm sure he never realized how much the rest of us leaned on him or how we found him to be a real force and example to us.

"I don't know," he said to me one day.

"Don't know what?"

"You know that Bible class I told you about—the one I want to start?"

"What about it?"

"I don't have the nerve."

"You?"

"I know the guys I want to ask, but I just don't have—the guts."

"How's your own Bible study going?" I asked.

"Not so well." He ran his hand through his hair. "I get it going for a week or so and then something comes up and I miss a day. It really bothers me."

You'd think the speakers who came to talk to us in chapel would have sensed our needs and temptations—as well as our potential. Bill used to say we got the saddest bunch of preachers you could scrape up in the whole USA. He had a good mind for cutting through the fat to get to the heart of the matter. I remember when the president of Yale spoke in our freshman year. He urged us to have a fixed purpose in life and to distinguish between right and wrong. Bill said that he neglected to say what our purpose should be and where we should get the ability to persevere and the strength to resist temptations—things we both felt were rather essential.

One night at a meeting of the Mission Volunteer Band, Ned Harvey spoke from Philippians 1:6, 9, and 10—you know, about God's part in our Christian life and about our part in having love that abounds in knowledge and judgment. We're to approve the things that are excellent and be sincere and without offense till the day of Christ.

When he was through, he said, "Anyone have

anything special to bring up?"

No one said anything.

Then Bill stood up. "I do," he said. Then opening his Bible he read James 5:16: "Confess your faults one to another, and pray one for another, that ye may be healed. The effectual fervent prayer of a righteous man availeth much."

Then he said, "I know I must learn to save people here before I can hope to save them anywhere else. I had such a good chance this afternoon to speak to a fellow. But I failed." Tears came to his eyes and started down his cheeks. "I want your prayers."

At another one of our band meetings, we got on the topic "Apart from me ye can do nothing." We all felt our need of God's help and the need to be more consecrated. One of the men admitted he wasn't wholly consecrated, and Bill confessed that too.

"But I want to be," he said.

James Howard, Bill, and I were chosen from the freshman class to be members of a personal workers' group. There were fourteen men in it from all the classes. We discussed opportunities we had to witness, and then we prayed for one another. We got to know some of the best men in the college. Bill often said a man's true friends are his Christian friends.

Bill went out for wrestling all four years. As a freshman, he fought in the middle-heavyweight class. In one meet he wrestled a senior and engaged in two bouts of five minutes each. Neither could put the other down, so they rested and then went at it again. After forty-nine minutes, the senior finally got Bill down. I know he lost three pounds in the process.

One of the big events of our freshman year was

the missionary convention of the Student Volunteer Movement, which was held in Nashville. More than four thousand delegates from colleges all over the country attended. I was not one of those chosen—I didn't have the money, either.

The last night before the delegation was to leave, I was in bed and almost asleep when a number of upperclassmen filed into my room. I believe Bill was with them.

"Hey, sleepy-head, what do you mean by going to bed? The night's young."

"For owls maybe," I yawned. "What's up?"

"Well, we've got great news for you, Charlie, old boy," one of the seniors said. "We need one more delegate, and we want you to go."

"But I don't have the—"

"All expenses paid, dummy. Someone made a donation that covers it."

Of course, I went. But I always had a feeling that Bill was behind that. If not, it was the kind of thing he was always doing while staying behind the scenes himself.

What a time we had on that long train journey to Nashville! We adjourned to the baggage car occasionally to let off steam with games that usually came from Bill's fertile imagination.

"Let's play 'hot hands,'" he said one time.

"What's that?"

"I saw some sailors on a German steamer play it. One man faces the side of the ship with his eyes closed and leans his head against the wall. Then the others go behind him and one of them gives him a whack. Nobody lets on who did it. The guy getting hit turns around quickly and tries to guess who hit him. If his guess is correct, he changes places with the whacker. If it isn't, he continues to get whacked until he guesses right."

Boy, did that game go over. And, as you might expect, Bill excelled in whacking and guessing.

Then we had high-kicking contests and wrestling and other games—all in the rapidly moving baggage car.

And so we reached Nashville, full of life and spirits. We separated there for the different homes in which we were to be entertained. Those were days of wonderful inspiration. And I can tell you this, if Bill was the one responsible for my going to Nashville, then he's the one who will get the reward. God used that experience to bring me a step further on in Christ. It was there that I gave my life to God in consecration for any work to which He might call me.

Foreign missionaries representing twenty-six countries spoke at the conference, but only one stood out to Bill and me. He had only a map and a burning passion for Christ. He was full of facts and enthusiasm, but deadly sincere. Samuel Zwemer made that map speak. Its appeal was the 200 million people in the Mohammedan world—200 million souls under the sway of Islam.

"No bondage on earth is more relentless," he said, "more deadening, and to its women more degrading. From China to the west coast of Africa and from the steppes of Russia right down to Zanzibar stretches the sweep of its influence and control. Only from scattered outposts is any Christian light spreading."

"Now is the time—the hour is ripe to reach them" was his message, and he preached it with startling facts. Telling us what missionaries were doing in Moslem lands, he pointed out country after country, province after province that was still absolutely without the Light of Life. Afghanistan with its four million Moslems had no missionaries at all. Some had missionaries among their heathen races, as in China, but none for the followers of the prophet. Not one missionary had been set apart to minister to China's fifteen million Moslems—and the door was not closed to the inland provinces where they lived.

Dr. Zwemer urged that we ought to press in, sacrificing our lives if need be for God, as the Moslems did at Khartum for their prophet. If the call voiced by those who had already spoken moved us deeply—missionaries who had come from Persia, from Turkey, from Egypt, from India—what could be said of the mute appeal of seventy million entirely unevangelized Moslems?

He asked, "Will we stand by and allow these seventy million people to continue under the curse and in the snare of a false religion with no knowledge of the saving love and power of Christ? It's not that they have proved fanatical and refused to listen, nor because they have thrust us back—they are lost because none of us has ever had the courage to go to those lands and win them to Jesus Christ.

"Of course, it will cost life. It's not an expedition of ease, nor a picnic excursion. It's going to cost many lives—and not lives only, but prayers and tears and blood."

He told us about Raymond Lull, the first missionary to the Moslems, who was stoned to death in Algiers. He told us about Henry Martyn, who pioneered in Persia with the cry, "Let me burn out for God."

"We who are missionaries to Moslems today," he said, "call upon you to follow with us in their train, to go to these waiting lands and light the beacon of the love of Christ in all the Mohammedan world. Did He not live, pray, suffer for Moslems as well as for us? Shall we do less if the call comes? Let us be like those Scots of Bruce who were ready to falter until that man on the white charger took the heart of Bruce in its casket and, swinging it round, cried out, 'Oh, heart of Bruce, lead on!' As he flung it toward the enemy and bore down upon them, you could not have held those soldiers back with bands of steel.

"Say not it is the appeal of the Mohammedan world or of the missionaries—it is the call of the Master. Let us answer with the shout, 'Oh, heart of Christ, lead on!' And we will follow that cry and win the Mohammedan world for Him."

He said there were more Moslems in China than there are in Persia. More in China than in the whole of Egypt, more in China even than in Arabia—the home and cradle of Islam. And he said there is *no one* giving himself to their evangelization!

"We do not plead for missions," he said, "we simply bring the facts before you and ask for a verdict." Then he quoted Proverbs 24:11-12: "If thou forbear to deliver them that are drawn unto death, and those that are ready to be slain; if thou sayest, Behold we knew it not; doth not he that pondereth the heart consider it? and he that keepeth thy soul, doth not he know it? and shall not he render to every man according to his works?"

Bill left Nashville committed in heart to taking the gospel to the Mohammedan world if the Lord should confirm that call. Oh, he didn't say much about it, but his best friends knew he was seriously considering working among Moslems in some unoccupied field.

Of course, those of us who went to Nashville were able to share what happened there with others. I shared a meeting with Bill and Ken Latourette, a senior. Bill felt bad later. He thought he'd done poorly. "There was a little pride and ambition inside me," he said. The rest of us thought he did fine.

In April we had an unexpected blow. The faculty let a student in without making him provide moral references. He got in with the wrong bunch and led a fast life. Then he got sick and went into the infirmary with pleurisy, pneumonia, and water on the heart.

Bill said he'd been meaning to get hold of him for the Lord but had never done anything. Few of us knew his sickness was serious until the rumor went out that he was dying. Bill and Bill Williams and I went to the infirmary to find the truth and were told he was unconscious and not likely to live out the day. We went right back to Borden's room and prayed. There was nothing we could do. That was at two o'clock. He died at three—we don't know whether he regained consciousness or not. It was an awful lesson to all three of us, and it should have made the whole university stop and think; but in no time the thing was forgotten.

However, Bill appointed a committee to draw up a resolution to send from our class to the boy's family. We sent flowers and wore mourning buttons for a month. Bill and I decided we really wanted to witness to some of those fast fellows for the Lord. Bill went up to see a few one night and found them playing cards with poker chips on the table. One of the men I'd been working with was in this crowd and he avoided me at first, but soon the Lord began to work in his heart.

We had another unexpected blow just after that. Bill's folks came for a visit on their way back home from Vassar where they'd heard their daughter Mary debate. It was the first time Bill's dad had visited either of his sons at school or college.

Arriving back in Chicago, he seemed perfectly well. But one Saturday evening he was taken sick, and on Sunday became critically ill. John and Bill were summoned home. Mary got there Monday evening in time to see him, though he was unconscious. Bill and John arrived on Tuesday morning, three or four hours after he had passed away.

Bill was only eighteen, but I could sense the resolve in his heart to be the man his mother would now need at her side. He began writing her every day.

There was never a time during those years when Bill was not looking for the opportunity to do personal work. He used the Bible study he had finally started to reach different ones. He and Farrand Williams worked with an earnest-minded agnostic. Once the two of them intercepted a fellow who had been expelled from the Hill School and kept him from carousing. They used physical force to stop him from following some women and walked him home, then prayed with him before they let him go.

Bill also worked with someone he called his "skeptical friend," and with another who doubted the immortality of the soul. Bill and Farrand and I were out walking one evening when a town fellow, half-drunk, swore at us. I asked him if he knew who the Christ was he'd just spoken about. Well, this started things, and we eventually brought him back to Bill's room. He seemed to be under conviction, but he wouldn't take any definite action to receive the Lord. We filled him up with water so he wouldn't want any more liquor. He promised he would come see us again.

The Yale Summer Conference followed commencement our first year; of course Bill and the rest of our bunch went. The college wanted to expand Bill's idea of small separate Bible study groups through all the classes. Someone made a canvass and found 150 men who expressed an interest. So part of the curriculum for the conference involved methods of conducting a small group Bible study.

S. D. Gordon, the author of so many books on prayer and power, spoke there. He pointed out to us that the world is intent on receiving things, each man getting what he wants. The preposition of man is *into* and that turns him into a Dead Sea—there's no outlet. But the preposition of Christ is *out of*—"*out of him shall flow rivers of living water.*"

Bill wrote this in his notebook after Sunday's talks:

> Say "No" to self, "Yes" to Jesus every time. A steep road—hard work? But every man on this road has One who walks with him in lock-step; His presence overtops everything that has been cut out . . .
>
> In every man's heart there is a throne and a cross. If Christ is on the throne, self is on the cross; and if self, even a little bit, is on the throne, Jesus is on the cross in that man's heart . . . If Jesus is on the throne, you will go where He wants you to go. Jesus on the throne glorifies any work or spot . . .
>
> If you are thirsty, and He is enthroned, *drink.* Drinking, the simplest act there is, means taking. "He

that believeth on Me, out of him shall flow rivers of living water. This spake He of the Spirit." To "believe" is *to know,* because of His word. How shall I know that I have power to meet temptation, to witness for Him? Believe His word: It will come.

Lord Jesus, I take hands off, as far as my life is concerned. I put Thee on the throne in my heart. Change, cleanse, use me as Thou shalt choose. I take the full power of Thy Holy Spirit. I thank Thee.

I may never know a tithe of the result until Morning.

4

Charlie Campbell (Cont.)

We saw all through the next year how those living waters would flow through Bill and out into blessings for many others.

One of the first decisions he had to make when we returned to school for our sophomore year was what he would do about the fraternities. Everyone at Yale—everyone who is anyone—points toward a frat. But for Bill it was no simple question.

Shortly before college opened, he asked James M. Howard, E. F. Jefferson, and me to come to Poughkeepsie to discuss the society question. His mother had taken a house near Vassar College where she could be near Mary, who was in her senior year.

Our discussion centered on two questions: Could we as Christians join a secret society? Would such action harm or help our work for Christ? Those were new thoughts to most of us. We had taken the society system very much for granted and had never questioned whether it was right or wrong for us to join one of the fraternities. But Bill took nothing for granted. He was a servant of Jesus Christ, and everything had to be tested and bear the stamp of Christ's approval before he would enter upon it.

The element of secrecy was one of Bill's difficulties with joining a fraternity. As a Christian he felt he should not go into anything that he did not clearly understand. He feared that the fraternity system led to the forming of cliques in the college. He didn't wish to be set apart from the class. Further, he didn't wish to have anything come between God and him. He had given himself wholeheartedly to Christ, to be His follower pure and simple, and he wanted that relation always kept real. Therefore, he felt he had no right to vow allegiance to any secret, man-made organization.

We didn't come to any conclusion then. After all, we still had a month to think it over once school started. Before that time, something happened that surprised all four of us. At Yale, during our time, each class chose four men at the beginning of their sophomore year who would act as deacons in the University Church. They would be charged with the responsibility for the religious work of their class.

The day of the elections we prayed together that God would guide the choice, so that the right people would be appointed. As it turned out, the four of us were chosen! We used to laugh about that.

Bill finally decided that he would join no fraternity. The other three of us did—in fact, we were among the first ones chosen. We felt we would have opportunities to witness we wouldn't have otherwise. I know for a fact that Bill lost some sleep over the matter. He's not all iron and steel. He wanted to join more than he let on, but he was standing for a principle, and he felt he couldn't budge.

Looking back now, it's obvious he was right. He had more influence with his class and with the underclassmen than he would have had otherwise.

He had more time, too. He did join the Elihu Club, an open organization, at the close of his junior year.

We didn't know it at that time, but his decision not to tie himself up with a fraternity freed him for ministry none of us ever anticipated.

On Bill's nineteenth birthday, the first of November, John Magee, the graduate secretary of the YMCA, pulled him aside. Bill told me about it later.

"Have you ever been down to the docks here in New Haven, Bill?"

"Why, yes, sir—a lot of times."

"What do you see there?"

"Oh, a lot of men milling about."

"There's work to be had on the docks," John said.

"It's a kind of way station, isn't it, for tramps and hoboes? I've seen a lot of them down there."

"And it's where the county jail is. A lot of prisoners are constantly being discharged, and there's no one down there to give them a helping hand."

"I've thought about that," Bill said.

"It seems to me," John paused, "that someone should extend that helping hand."

"Right."

"But I see more than just meeting the needs of the down-and-out. I see the possibility of opening a rescue mission with its doors always open. You know, like they have in New York."

"You mean Jerry McAuley's Water Street Mission?"

"I do. And I think it could serve us a double purpose."

"What's that?"

"I can't think of any better witness to the men on this campus to the saving power of Jesus Christ than to have a place in this city where hopeless sinners are being converted and made new."

"Great idea! When do we start?"

"We've got to pray about it first," John said.

"Oh, I know that. It's just that it seems like just what we've wanted to do all along—give these students an object lesson of God's power to change men. I've got a few skeptic friends I could take down there right now and let them see the Spirit of God really at work saving souls."

A week later Bill and John met with two converted drunkards, a Mr. Skinner and old Brother Martin, to talk over plans for the mission. They decided to pray for another week to see what would develop. In February special meetings featured a Mr. Mercer, who opened the eyes of the men on campus to the evils of social drinking. The "glass" had ruined him when he was a student at the University of Virginia.

Everything was finally ready in mid-March. A room had been rented in a cheap hotel in just the right quarter. It had hideous dark red wallpaper. Later, Bill bought the entire building, and installed downstairs dormitories and shower baths and a place in which clothes could be fumigated. Upstairs it offered a good, inexpensive lodging-house known as the Hotel Martin—named after old Brother Martin. For two dollars a week a man could have a room to himself.

We carted hymnbooks in my suitcase down to the hall for that first meeting. The handle of the suitcase broke and we had to hoist it on our shoulders and carry it through the streets. Bill was heart and soul in that work. It was great to see him—so earnest in his presentation of the truth and in dealing with those who came forward for prayer.

Afterwards, he would often help the men find a place to sleep. He would pay the lodging-house charge himself to avoid putting temptation in their way by giving them money.

They got a Mr. Bernhardt to take over the full-time management of what they called the Yale Hope Mission. He was a graduate of the University of Georgia and had done his post-graduate work at Vanderbilt. He had risen to the position of cashier in a big southern express company. Then, through gambling, he got into debt, which led to stealing and, ultimately, to prison. He entered an innocent boy, but left a hardened criminal. It wasn't until he had completed twenty-two years in prison that he "lost his nerve" and determined to be a man. After being released, he traveled eight thousand miles searching for work.

Finally, stranded in New York, he decided to take his life. On his way to the river he heard singing from the Water Street Mission and investigated. Nothing happened that night or the next, but on the third night the great change came and he received the Lord. He was mightily used of God from the first at the Yale Hope Mission. Eight men came forward, several in dead earnest, the first night he preached.

5

Charlie Campbell (Cont.)

None of us realized in our junior year that Bill had only five more years to live. That year, he chose a room in White Hall on Berkeley Oval, just off the old college campus. Malcolm B. Vilas of Cleveland was his roommate. He was a boy of fine character who had taken a positive Christian stand at the Lakeville Conference at the close of our freshman year. I lived next door with Louis G. Audette, and across the way were two other classmates, Sandford D. Stockton and Frank Assman. It was a great combination, made up of very different types—and what times we did have! Every now and then we would get rid of extra energy in a big roughhouse. We would nag at Bill until we had him roused, and then he would get started. Around that room he would go like a tornado, crushing all opposition. It was a sight to see him really roused. He was a fellow of unusual physical strength and knew how to use it to his advantage. I found that the best way to treat Bill when he went at me was to give right in. This seemed to mollify him, while resistance only spurred him on to greater efforts. We used to have many a tussle, but he was altogether too strong for the average man. And with his knowledge of wrestling, he was more than a match for any of us. We would laugh at him because of his strength and call him a "brute."

The activities of the religious work went along much the same. There were the Bible groups, the mission study classes, the daily prayer groups, the Wednesday evening Bible classes, the Volunteer Band meetings, and the Yale Hope Mission—all of which occupied Bill's time. The latter was especially absorbing for Bill that year. I believe he took one night a week at the Mission to conduct the service.

During our Christmas vacation, Bill went with his mother and Joyce to the Lake Placid Club in the Adirondacks. It was a beautiful winter with several feet of snow on the ground in the mountains. Bill and his mother, with their willing hospitality, decided to have a house-party. Invitations came to Isabel Corbiere, Mary Abbe, and three of my sisters; Mac Vilas, Bill Roberts, Lou Audette, and myself. All but Mac Vilas were able to accept, and we arrived on New Year's Eve.

How crisp the mountain air was as we drove up in sleighs from the station and started in for a glorious party. We cast off all thought of work and settled down to healthy outdoor sport. Bill, of course, was in the thick of it. We would all dress up in our warmest old clothes and go out to the toboggan course. The snow was soft, so all kinds of stunts were possible. We spent a good deal of time trying to go down the hill standing on the toboggans. Four or five of us would get on one and launch out. There always came the time when someone would lose his balance and upset the rest, and away we would go—head first into the snow. It was fine healthy sport, and Bill was right in his element.

Over on the road, coasting on the bobsled was possible, and near the club the skating was great. One day we all ploughed off in the deep snow and climbed a little mountain near by. Every night we would turn up tired, healthily so, and ready for the biggest dinner and the soundest sleep. Bill simply reveled in good fellowship and sport, and it did one good to be with him. He made an ideal host and always saw that his guests had a good time.

Later that winter, Mrs. Borden's health deteriorated. She moved to New Haven to be near Bill. He became so busy that she might have lost track of him if she had not been close by. He was president of Phi Beta Kappa and was active in football, baseball, crew, and wrestling. He rowed on the winning 1909 club crew in the fall of his junior year and played on both the winning Philosophical and High Oration as well as the Phi Beta Kappa baseball teams. He served on the class book committee and on the senior council, was a class deacon, and was more than willing to do his share of the drudgery for the good of his class. He was chairman of the Student Missionary Union of colleges in the Connecticut Valley and made all the arrangements for the annual conference.

At the Phi Beta Kappa banquet in the winter of 1908, Bill, as president of the society, took the lead. The Phi Beta Kappa banquet is perhaps the finest of the yearly banquets given at Yale. Many celebrated men from other colleges and most of the best known professors of the university are invited, so the dinner is quite an affair. I have a pleasant recollection of the dignified way in which Bill presided and made the opening address. It was a striking illustration of his maturity and balance.

When the class book came out, Bill received several accolades: voted third for being "the hardest worker"; fourth among "the most energetic"; ninth as "the most to be admired"; and seventh in the vote for "the one who had done the most for Yale." Bill's class numbered nearly three hundred.

But, you know, for Bill, prayer was his most important work. It was the breath of his life. He had a card system for recording prayer requests and answers concerning individuals who were on his heart. He had a loose-leaf notebook in which he listed subjects for prayer in columns, one for each day of the week. The scope of those notes even for one day is a revelation of the depth and thoroughness of the prayer life they represented—reaching out to the ends of the earth.

Through all the time I knew him, when there was opportunity, we never parted without going on our knees and praying for God's work.

One of our friends said of Bill, "How easy he was to pray with. He was a jolly fellow—loved a roughhouse—delighted to get hold of a man and crack his ribs. He could be jolly with the rest; yet, when the crowd was gone, it would be just as natural for him to say, 'Come into the bedroom and let us have prayer together.'

"There was no sense of incongruity about it. I remember very vividly—how could one ever forget—those times of prayer when just the two of us would kneel down and take to God some of the problems we were facing. Bill was so simple in his prayer life, so natural, so trustful. He was the easiest man to pray with I have ever known."

One of the passions of Bill's life was righteousness.

He hungered for it. He thirsted for it. His prayer life was full of petitions that illustrated this, and his actual living illustrated it too. I remember that after we had finished our final examinations our senior year, we had a four day interval before commencement. Bill, with a few others of us, ran up to his place in Maine and attempted to sail his boat down to New Haven. We had head winds all the way and could do no better than reach Cape Cod and put in to Hyannisport in time to take a train to New Haven. As we walked up the streets of Hyannisport, where Bill had spent a summer as a boy, he remembered that at the close of that vacation he had gone away owing some shopkeeper in the place a few cents. He had forgotten all about it, but it came back to him as we walked up the street that day. He insisted on finding the little shop and paying the debt so that he might be straight with the world. That was his nature—if he found anything wrong with his life, he set to work to make it right.

But there was another characteristic of Bill's life, and that was his great loving heart, which always seemed to me his richest and rarest quality. There were many, perhaps, who, seeing him in a casual way busy with the work he had to do, set him down as severe and unapproachable. We know that the very opposite was true. He had one of the most affectionate, lovable natures of any man I have ever known. No one who visited his home could for a moment doubt this. And I mean more than family love—he had a way, for example, when walking with a friend, of putting his arm over his shoulder as they talked. I can feel the great loving touch of his arm about my shoulder even now.

After graduation we attended Northfield again,

sleeping in a tent as before. For two summers Bill waited tables during the conference. He never did this if there was a man needing the job to help make expenses. But if the coast was clear, on would go the waiter's apron and he would do the work, getting nothing to eat himself until the crowd had left the dining room. He never told me why he did this. It may have been partly to keep friends company who had to wait tables for monetary reasons. But I always felt it went deeper than that, that Bill was trying to be among us as "he that serveth."

6

Jack Clark

(A man Bill led to Christ at Yale Hope Mission)

I came in here to the Yale Hope Mission on the twenty-seventh of March, 1908. I was on a drunk and hadn't much use for religion. I'm not going to tell the worst part of my life, but I was a rambler all right—a down-and-out bum. There was only three states in the Union I hadn't been in. I had heard of the Mission, same as a good many of them do. I knew it was the only thing that would save me from booze. Well, I went out, that first night. I had a Christian mother, and I got to thinking of her, so I came back. That was the twenty-ninth, and that night Bill was there, and he spoke to me. Bill was a great personal worker—he always believed in getting right down and talking to a man. If Bill had anything to say, he gave it right out. I know the gist of what he said to me that night.

"What are you going to do about it? Can't you see where you've missed the road?"

He would tell you to hope again; tell you of how God, who'd made the universe and held you in the hollow of His hand, could help you if you'd only ask. That's the way he talked. He was one good boy. I could never forget him as long as I breathe—no, I never forget him. And he was barely twenty that night I first knew him! He was at Yale College then, and Louis Bernhardt was superintendent of the mission.

I went forward and kneeled down and Bill came and kneeled down beside me. He explained as much as he could about the power of Jesus Christ, and how it was only Him who could help me. I never drank from that night to this, never felt like it—never felt like it, from the twenty-ninth day of March, 1908, to this. Before that I was drunk most of the time—I had been drunk all that winter. Bill was a great man to watch you and not say much, but just ask how you were getting along. Well, after I was converted I come every night—didn't miss a night after that for seven weeks.

It's all fresh in my mind yet. I got work soon, too. I got a job on an ice wagon. That was one of the greatest tests on the boozing that I ever got. I was boss of the team that year and went back and was boss again the second summer. I was boss sixteen or seventeen months altogether. I hadn't worked only three weeks when they put me in charge of the team.

I saw Bill right along those times, except in his vacation—he was in Europe then. And he wrote me a letter. After some time I went back to the shop, and then I was foreman in the New Haven County Jail, where I'd served time in a cell. About two years after I was converted, I was remarried right in this building, right upstairs. I think Bill sent a letter that he couldn't come, but he knew I was going to be married. He met my wife and family—seemed tickled to death, too, to meet 'em. We've got a home now in Yalesville, Connecticut, and a big garden—

plenty of land, lots of chickens, and a piano in the house. It makes quite a change from when I first came to the mission, drunk, with no prospects but whiskey! There's not been a day since my conversion that I haven't had money in my pocket, not a day from that day to this. God has wonderfully blessed me.

After my conversion, I was baptized and joined the church. If Bill hadn't opened this mission, I'd been dead by now.

My old chum who was once on the bum with me, he'd never have been converted if it hadn't been for this mission. We was holding prayer meetings at different houses. They'd come in drunk sometimes. Then I always took 'em after the meetings and gave 'em a talking to just before they left. Told 'em about this work here at Yale Hope Mission. There's no time in a drunkard's life when he don't have serious thoughts. When he drowns his conscience in booze, he's tearing away from the voice of God, I think.

Well, someone asked my chum to come when the meeting was at my house. He said he would if Jack Clark would lead. He knew that what God did for Jack Clark, God could do for him. There was about twenty-four there, and I led. That night Whitney Todd, my chum, was converted. He lives right in Yalesville now and is foreman of a shop. He's got his wife and children with him, and he's always got his hand out to the man that's down. So you see, you cannot trace what Yale Hope Mission's done by what you see lying around. Not till the books of Heaven are opened will you know what Bill Borden done by opening Yale Hope Mission.

He was great at individual work. As a talker, he'd hasten through his address and get to work with the men, always aiming to get close to the man he was talking with—always with his hand on his shoulder. He didn't believe in talking over people's heads, but tried to land right on his man and bring his thoughts right home. He would interest you quicker than the ordinary man, because he had a more sympathetic way. He seemed to reach out and win you. I watched him some nights, and always, as soon as the invitation was given to come forward, he would be off the platform and right down among the men, urging them to accept a better life. He was always sympathetic, and he never went at a man in the same way twice. They'd most always break down when he spoke to them.

I never knew a feller just like Bill. I'd like to get a hold of one of his pictures. Seems to me if I saw one I'd 'most try to steal it. He was a gentleman in every sense of the word, and a Christian through and through. That was first and last in his life. He enjoyed life, and people who came in contact with him, seeing his happy spirit, would say, "Why, life is worth living after all."

The way he came amongst us, you would never think he was a man of wealth—he always dressed so plain. He had a peculiar way, very interesting to me. He wouldn't tell you anything about himself, but he had a way of making you talk and tell things. It seemed to be his whole object, to know how I was and about my life so as he could help. It couldn't seem possible a man could be so humble and yet so great. He could talk to anyone, didn't matter who they was. And he'd get down with his arms round the poor burly bum and hug him up.

I know he must have done for hundreds just what he done for me.

E. F. ("Pop") Jefferson

No picture of Bill at New Haven would be complete without the old slouch hat he used to wear so often. Remember it? It was a brownish gray, pointed at the top, torn on the side, and with a large convenient hole he used to hang it up by.

One time, I set fire to Bill's hat. When he discovered the flame, he was suddenly active to rescue the treasure and punish me for my presumption.

You'd think he would have thrown it away after that. He didn't.

7

Captain Arey

(Captain of the Borden family yacht)

William was a nice hand to sail a boat. You didn't need no one else when he was along. I used to be afraid he'd fall in the water, at first. He was always singin' and jumpin' around. He'd climb away up the riggin' and get into the rowboat behind. He did everything well he tried to do. He was so strong, too! When he'd go out and work at the riggin', I'd be afraid he'd break the sail, he was so strong. Sometimes he'd steer and sometimes he'd help with the sails, but he was an expert on the boat. He could take a chart and go anywhere with it. Of course, he'd studied into it and learned it. It didn't seem hard for him to go through with anything he undertook—it just seemed easy.

I'd known Bill ever since he first come to Camden, and that must have been around 1904. If anyone showed on their outside the happiness of being a Christian, it was William Borden. When he talked, it just seemed as if you could feel his earnestness.

When we two was out alone—we went all the way to New Haven alone once—I've seen him kneel for perhaps an hour at a time and never lift his head.

The villagers loved him; everybody loved him. He was so noble-looking! When he came up in the spring, he always shook hands with everybody. All the summer people don't do that. If 'twas a stranger or a fisherman, didn't make no difference. He always spoke to everybody, like as if he wanted to, and shook hands with them.

One awful good feature he had: if the boat wasn't fixed up quite as it ought to be, perhaps if ladies came aboard and the brass wasn't cleaned, I'd tell him about it, and he'd smile and say it was all right. He never spoke a cross word to me all the time I was with him.

He lent me two books by Gordon, *Talks on Prayer* and *Talks on Power.* We had a young people's meeting in the Baptist church here. After the summer in London when he was converted, he would sometimes lead our prayer meeting. If I had the job, I'd get him to do it for me. Others did too, for they liked to hear him. He could always hold the audience. Sometimes the young people was a little noisy at their meeting, but they was still when he spoke.

Sometimes he'd tell us he was going to be a missionary—seemed to think he was mapped out for it. If 'twas worldly pleasure he'd wanted, he could have had everything. But he was so much different from others! All his pleasure seemed to be in going about doin' people good. The last summer here at one of the meetin's he said he was going to the Mohammedans. He spoke about the National Bible Institute one night but I don't remember just what he said.

If we was out all night on the boat, he'd roll in the blanket and sleep on deck. The others would be in the cabin. There might be a bed to spare, but he'd take the deck—he liked it better.

One summer here, he and Mr. T. held open-air meetings. They'd begin right in front of the hotel, about half past seven, and get the crowds sort of interested. They had a little organ and would sing. William could sing quite well. He had a strong voice. Then they'd go into the opera house, which they'd rented for a while. Sometimes it was crowded full. The last two evenings they'd have after-meetin's, and many stayed. After the meetin' was opened—in the opera house—anybody could speak. Many did. The superintendent of the mills spoke one night, and sometimes ministers would come and speak.

It was blowin' awful heavy one night—dark and rainy. Two other fellers was out with us, his friends. About two o'clock in the mornin', the bran' new boat we was towin', the steam-launch—rolled over and sunk. The rope parted. I remember what he said.

"The boat's gone," he called down to the other fellers. "We can go faster now."

Lots and lots of boats that night that was about as big as the *Tsatsawassa,* our boat, was wrecked—that is, the sails was torn and the spars broke, so that they had to be towed in. The storm commenced about eleven o'clock. James Perry and another of William's friends was with us. I don't think any of us slept. I know I didn't, and I know William didn't. It was about six o'clock next mornin' when we got into Beverley Farms and anchored (after a record run of nearly two hundred miles in eighteen hours). When all was made safe, William said, "Now we'll have family prayers and give thanks for gettin' in."

He always had prayers for us every mornin'. Whoever was on the boat, we always had prayers and a blessin' at table. Sometimes she'd be so keeled over that we'd be standin' up, but that didn't make no difference. We always had a blessin'. If we was in port Sunday mornin', we'd go ashore to church. Perhaps I'd stay aboard—someone had to be there. But before he'd go ashore, he'd have prayers with me on the boat. He was always thoughtful, that way, of others. If he'd been my own brother, he couldn't have used me any better.

Once he and his sister Mary was out, and a fog and heavy sea came on. We couldn't get back to the landing stage, so they went to my house and stayed all night.

He just said so natural-like to my wife, "Have you anything to eat? We didn't get much supper. Can you give us some milk and cake?"

My wife went to all the meetin's. She liked him, too. He wasn't like one of the summer people. I'd be awful glad to have his picture, so'd my wife.

When he and I'd go out alone sometimes, I'd ask where he'd like to go.

"Anywhere," he'd say, "so as to get out where it's quiet."

And he'd go down into the cabin with his Bible or some other book and study all the time we was out. It might be three hours or so. And when we'd come in, he'd seem to be kind of refreshed in his mind.

He always read the Bible before turnin' in at night. It didn't matter who was there. If I was alone with him, he'd read it to me and explain it. Yes, he was jolly, and he was happy in the work he was undertakin'.

His mother asked me once what he was like when he was off duty—you know, off his guard.

I told her, "Mrs. Borden, William was never off his guard."

He was as steady in his allegiance to God as the needle to the pole.

Mrs. Sherwood Day

(A close family friend)

In the very first conversation I ever had with Bill, we discovered that we both believed in the inerrancy of the Bible, and I can feel yet the hearty grasp of his outstretched hand as we laughed in serious sympathy over our common orthodoxy!

That was the summer he joined us at Shelving Rock. I had hesitated to invite him, because it was real camping; and I fancied he might need some conveniences which are no longer considered luxuries, but necessaries.

I soon learned, however, that comforts were easily dispensable with him and that no change of surroundings interfered with his habitual walk with God.

That same summer Harriet, my daughter, was with us. She dubbed him "the Parson" and remembers the amused little smile with which he responded to her fun. They too frolicked together so much that I remember Sherwood's saying, "I wish the college fellows could see this side of Bill."

We knew that he went in for athletics and outdoor life, but until then it seemed as if even they were serious undertakings with him. But with Harriet, the playful side of him was brought out, and we were so glad to know the boy under the manly exterior.

Harriet Day

(Mrs. Day's daughter)

I, too, loved his standing simply and firmly for the eternal verities of our faith. That staunchness of his after all his thought and study has meant much to me. And I have learned much, too, from the way Bill stood for truth. We always noticed that the more earnest he became, the lower, not the louder, he spoke. When others in argument would raise their voices, he would grow quieter and speak lower, with the result that everyone listened.

I recall one day a heated discussion of the suffrage question. Mother used Genesis as her basis against it. One of our pro-suffrage guests did not accept that because he denied much belief in Genesis, anyway.

I don't remember that up to that point Bill had said much, but somehow, the first thing I knew, he was talking along, and the other guests were listening. Much that he said was beyond us; we did not know enough to follow it fully. But the impression was made that one can have a deep scholarly conviction in the authority and inspiration of the Scriptures, and that one need not be an *unthinking* conservative, but simply an intelligent believer in the Bible.

I do not know that he convinced the friends in question—they did not talk long. But he did what I felt at the time was perhaps more needed: he showed that we could hold to the old views in these matters, after thinking. Real certainty and security in the truth is unruffled when attacks come. He was so sure of what he believed—in Whom he believed—that he did not get excited and loudly insist on his opinions. He could wait to say what he *knew.* And the more you knew him the more sure you felt that, keen and active as his intellect was, his knowledge was the result of no mere theological training, but of personal experience and prayerful Spirit-guided study of the Word of God.

The thought of him always challenges me. One knew that he was holding himself and always would hold himself to what he felt to be best and highest. He would not stoop to petty excuses or take advantage of loopholes for self-indulgence. Here at camp he was up early for his morning watch as regularly as, I am sure, he must have been at the seminary. I can see his Testament coming out of his pocket now. As surely as he carried that Book, he carried his religion. You felt he would never be one to want a vacation from religious duties, because they were not "duties" to him. It was just natural for him to take that morning hour for fellowship with God—and he bore its imprint all through the day.

It was always an opportune time to speak with Bill of the deepest things, because with him they were the realest things. His spiritual life affected his entire life—the heartiness and wholesomeness of his fun as well as his religious activities.

If there arose in his mind a doubt about the

rightness of something, he put the doubtful thing aside at once. For example, he became very interested in a card game someone was playing here in camp and took some share in it. Then, one day he would not play it anymore, and you knew it was because he had questioned the rightness of his taking such a keen interest in the game. It was this steadfast turning from doubtful things that gave him, I think, the atmosphere of separateness that was part of his power.

And then, I suppose, the single-mindedness in his spiritual life was the secret that took him straight along from the point where he had set out. What Bill started you might be quite sure he would finish. From the room in which I write, I can see where a limb has been cut off a tree, high up from the ground. Bill cut it off. Someone expressed a wish that the dead limb might go because it looked like an ugly clenched fist, so he set out to do it. The ladder was not long enough—he had to prop it up. It was on a steep hillside, and dangerous. He had to hang on with his right arm and saw with his left in an almost impossible position. I can see him doing it now, sawing and resting and sawing again, but sticking at it until the limb fell.

There's one other thing I want to speak of, but I don't quite know how to describe it. It was something that made you feel that everything would be all right as long as he was around. It was partly, I suppose, his consideration for others.

When, one evening last September, Rosalie and I ran him down to the Sagamore so he could get an automobile for Lake George, he discovered that we had no flashlight in the launch with which to examine the engine if it should happen to stall on our way back. He insisted on giving us his, one from his traveling bag, because he felt we ought not to be without it. And as we started home leaving him there on the dock, he called out to us—novices at running the engine—not to forget about an oil cup, I think it was, that we should attend to.

He was such a one to rely on. And it seemed to me that his Lord's spirit of service had so permeated his life that it not only led him to set his face to the field of greatest need, but made his life full of little services, day by day, that many would not see the occasion for. It was easy to see his force, his devotion to Christ's cause, but it was only after having him around that you began to appreciate what a Christlike man he was.

Rosalie Day

(Mrs. Day's second daughter)

A kindness he did in a New York station is one of the things I have recalled repeatedly. We were going out to take a train, when I noticed that he had dropped behind, and, turning, I saw him helping a very poor immigrant woman who was struggling along with several bundles and a baby in her arms. I remember well at camp how he used to stand near the kitchen door and watch for a chance to be of use. We often said that the table was never cleared so quickly as when Bill did it.

And what a help he was with some German I had

to do for an examination at Bryn Mawr. The days at camp were pretty well filled with picnics, canoeing, swimming, so it was not easy to make time for study. He was anxious that I should finish that German reading. If a thing had to be done, it was his way to do it and then put it from his mind. When there were a few minutes before it was time to start on a picnic or other outing, he would say, "Can't we get some of that German done now?"

I do not know how I should ever have tackled it without this encouragement. His help during the few days he was there gave me a running start, so to speak, that enabled me to finish in the required time.

But with all his seriousness there was abundant playfulness and love of fun. He had an inexhaustible store of tricks, which kept us entertained many an evening. I remember especially a spelling game called "ghost" that he enjoyed immensely.

One other outstanding thing about Bill was his instant and full obedience to the will of God. There never seemed to be any conflict in his life between duty and pleasure; from the moment he saw what his duty was, he did it. There was no procrastination about him. If the thing was hard to do, it made no difference. Emotions were out of the reckoning. "Obedience irrespective of feeling" was, perhaps, the strongest thing about his life.

One of the most vivid memories I have of him is seeing him sitting before our open fire at camp one Sunday evening. We were all there singing hymns, and the only light was that of the fire which shone full on his face. How earnest it was and with what joyousness he sang the hymns he loved best. "O

Love That Will Not Let Me Go" and "In the Secret of His Presence" were among his favorites.

But it was not the firelight only that brought that light to his face.

Elsa Frost

(A close family friend)

His ideals and ambitions were so great that anyone who knew him at all could not but be influenced by them, and to us who counted ourselves friends of his they were much more.

My most vivid remembrance of William has not to do with any football game or sailing, but with a communion service we all attended together at Camden. I somehow think of him most often then—not that he did or said anything to fix it in my mind, but just that he seemed to be so in the spirit of the service. When at times I am tempted to wonder whether the end in view is worth all the work and struggle, thinking of the separations and hardships he was facing is enough to start me on again.

8

Charlie Campbell

Three of Bill's last four years were spent at Princeton Theological Seminary. Mrs. Borden rented a house near the campus so she and her daughter Joyce could see as much of him as possible. She still wasn't very strong, so the responsibility of keeping the household running, paying the servants, and being host fell to Bill. They always had lots of company, but that wasn't all that kept Bill busy.

I learned that Bill, then twenty-one, had charge of some of the financial interests of the family. He was also taking a full load of studies at the seminary. I don't know how he did it, except that he was very methodical. He knew what to do and when and how to do it. His studies were absorbing and his social life congenial. He was a member of the Benham Club, the oldest eating club of the seminary. He played most of the games but was especially fond of tennis. He was a leader among the Student Volunteers and was always present at the early morning prayer service of the Mission Band each Wednesday.

In addition to the duties and pleasures that centered on his life in the seminary, Bill had many responsibilities outside Princeton itself. In the fall of 1909 he had been made a trustee of the Moody Bible Institute of Chicago. In the spring of 1910 he was appointed a delegate to the Edinburgh Missionary Conference by the China Inland Mission, and in the fall was made one of the directors of the National Bible Institute of New York City. He also became a member of the North American Council of the China Inland Mission and of the American Committee of the Nile Mission Press.

It's easy to see why he would have so many opportunities. His singleness of purpose helped him and gave such direction to his life that no one, even among his nearest friends, saw anything but a quiet, consistent, unhurried execution of each task that came. Almost every month he went to New Haven to look over the work of the Yale Hope Mission. The unusual feature of his relationship to all such organizations was that he was never satisfied with merely giving generous financial aid—he always gave time, thought, and counsel. His New York, New Haven, and Chicago trips succeeded one another, and yet he never neglected his work, though he carried a much heavier schedule than the average man. And he stood very high in scholarship at the seminary.

His life at Princeton was brightened by the happy home influences that surrounded him. His home was hospitably open to all. Students, missionaries, and prominent lay workers were frequent visitors. The tennis court at the back of the house was the scene of many hotly contested games. In spite of his busy life, Bill never neglected his body—he made it a point to get an hour's exercise daily. How his eyes would light up at the prospect of a good game of tennis! Back he would come from a class, hustle into tennis clothes and then out to the court. He was never more than an average tennis player, but he played hard all the time and gave his opponent plenty of work.

Brenton Greene

(Professor, Princeton Seminary)

I used to think, as I saw him from my study window dashing down Library Place on his bicycle to the early morning recitations, *that man is so strong and so sane that his prospect of life is better than that of any other student in our seminary.*

His memory was as wax to receive an impression and as marble to retain it. He had the happy faculty of seeing at once the gist of a question and going straight to the point. Yet he never relied on this power but used every means at his command. Rarely if ever was he absent from the classes, and I cannot recall a single instance of inattention on his part. As might have been expected, he attained the natural result—he became distinguished as a scholar.

I well remember my deep regret, the feeling of loss, at the time of his graduation, when I read his last paper knowing that I should never have another from him.

Dr. Henry W. Frost

(Director in North America of the China Inland Mission)

I loved William. He was like a son to me. I knew him almost all his life. When he was twenty-two, I invited him to sit with me on the council of the China Inland Mission of which I was then director in North America.

The disparity in age between him and the other members of the council was seldom noticed. There was an equality of mind that made him one with those with whom he was associated. None could help notice the freshness of thought and enthusiasm of spirit characteristic of youth, but they were not accompanied by immaturity of judgment. When William spoke, it was evident that he was thinking carefully and broadly. He was a constant illustration of the fact that it is no vain thing for a man, even a young man, to obey the injunction, "If any of you lack wisdom, let him ask of God." Christ, through William's study of the Word and through prayer, was made unto him "wisdom." His advice, therefore, was sought by not a few who, in the average case, would have gone to the man of more years. His eagerness to be of assistance made him a greater help than the average man, even one more wise through experience, would have been.

The first time William spoke to me about offering himself to the China Inland Mission was while he was a sophomore at Yale. He had already come to feel that his work should be in China and desired to put himself in a position to reach that land. But I felt he was then too young to come to a positive conclusion concerning the country in which he should serve, so I advised him to postpone considering the matter.

At the end of his university course, he again consulted me about going to China. Once more I advised him to defer the decision and urged him to prepare himself further by taking the seminary course at Princeton. This he did, with credit to himself and to the seminary.

Toward the end of his studies at Princeton, he again offered himself to the mission for work in China. This time I was persuaded that God was indeed in the matter of his application. But to further test him I asked if he had considered offering himself to the Presbyterian Board rather than to us.

He replied that he had. He highly esteemed the Presbyterian Board, but there were three reasons why he was more drawn to the China Inland Mission—first, its interdenominational character; second, its emphasis upon evangelistic work; and third, its stand on the personal and premillennial coming of Christ. So at last we considered his application and accepted him for service in China.

When his case came up for final consideration, we had to ask him to withdraw while the council proceeded to accept one of its own members as a probationer of the mission.

In 1910, we sent him as a representative of the mission to the Ecumenical Missionary Conference in Edinburgh, Scotland, where he was the youngest of two thousand delegates. I understand that it was there that his mother learned for the first time that he was giving himself definitely to the work of

Mohammedans in China, if that proved to be the Lord's will.

After the conference, he traveled in Europe. He wrote me from Hanover, Germany, on July 20:

> Only today I read in a London paper: "Unity of Christendom—gigantic task! Twenty-four American Episcopalians have undertaken to bring about a union of Christians all over the world—Protestants, Greek Catholics, Roman Catholics, everybody, everywhere!" Things are certainly rushing to the climax. I wonder what will come next?
>
> People talk about peace Congresses, but in reality here in Europe they are preparing for a great struggle I believe . . . How wonderful that we have "that blessed hope" to look forward to, "the glorious appearing of our God and Savior Jesus Christ"!

Reverend James M'Cammon

(A fellow student at Princeton Seminary)

Bill's thoroughness, especially in his studies, was evident to us all. He kept up his work from day to day, so that he was not rushed as many of us were when examinations came round. So well did he have his knowledge in hand that long before the three hours' period for an exam was over he would have finished his paper and handed it in, to the plaudits of his fellow students.

It was my habit to look in on a classmate in Alexander Hall daily and there, two or three afternoons a week, I was sure to find Bill and his friend

Fowler doing extracurricular work on Arabic. On one such occasion I discovered they had decided to make an Arabic concordance of the Bible and had actually begun work on it. I had known of their studiousness before, but this more than astonished me.

He was one of the most faithful attendants we had at the YMCA and Student Volunteer meetings in the seminary. He took his turn in leading the meetings, and his messages were of a devotional and missionary character that evidenced thorough preparation of mind and heart. One term he presented the reports of the World's Missionary Conference, which he had attended in Edinburgh, giving them in the form of a synopsis week by week. Those talks I shall never forget. His mastery of the facts was astonishing. It was remarkable evidence of his knowledge as well as his zeal in connection with foreign missions.

He was a convinced believer in the personal and premillennial coming of our Lord. He looked for that glorious advent as the hope of the church and the only hope for the world. I often had conversations with him on that subject, and the extent of his knowledge and intensity of his convictions left their mark on my mind. One of my most prized possessions is a book on the Lord's coming that he once gave me as we were talking.

Another conviction that dominated his life was that the Bible, from first word to last, is the inspired Word of God. To him it was the Book of books. He had not only an intellectual grasp of its teachings as one may get in a theological seminary, but he had the spiritual understanding that only comes through prayerful and devotional study in humble dependence on the Spirit of God.

The secret of William Borden's life, as it seems to a fellow student, was his belief in the sufficiency and abiding presence of the Lord Jesus Christ. For him this was more than a belief—it was a reality.

9

Don O. Shelton

(President of National Bible Institute of New York)

Three years before I became closely involved with William Borden, the Lord laid an unusual burden on my heart. I'd worked twenty years with the Young Men's Christian Association and had preached God's Word in a Bible conference ministry. But the people who needed reaching were not in YMCA meetings and the like—more than half the people in the whole country never attended church. Of what value is preaching to empty seats when the people who ought to occupy them are in crowded tenements or on street corners or in the parks and do not hear the faintest whisper of the message?

Well, after much prayer and consideration, a number of businessmen in New York agreed to support a simple, earnest effort to reach the crowds that walk through the city on their lunch hour. We had our first meeting in June 1907, using a low platform under a tree in Madison Square Garden. We had a little organ and a group of singers to lead the singing of familiar hymns. The speakers were businessmen. Their language was that of the newspaper, not the theology book. And the results were amazing. We would see three hundred men, with their attention riveted on our speaker, standing through our daily half-hour service. More men assembled daily to hear the message than gathered on Sundays for almost any Protestant church service in Greater New York. And what throngs we had—workingmen from nearby buildings, clerks from offices, bootblacks sitting on their kits; street cleaners, messenger boys, police officers, contractors, well-to-do businessmen, drunkards; the unemployed and discouraged, editors and professional people—all listening with the same interest.

We never took a collection. The one object was to reach men, and from the beginning we had crowds of them. The work thus far has resulted in many transformations of character. Some of those who have been helped expressed their purpose to unite with churches at once. We believe that we are carrying out Christ's charge to the people and not waiting for them to come to us.

Well, this seemed to catch the interest of Mr. Borden. He had been one of the founders of the Yale Hope Mission in New Haven, and he was interested in reaching the souls of men. He was only twenty-two years old and a student at Princeton Seminary when I first met him. As he became more familiar with the work, he became more interested. Something sparked between us, and we became good friends.

I went to see him off on the ship the summer he went to the Edinburgh conference as a representative of the China Inland Mission. There on the steamer, with all the noise and excitement going on around us, he pulled me to one side.

"I want to help you in the work you are doing," he said. "I will send you a hundred dollars a month for the next year. If you will come to my cabin, I will write the first check now."

Well, we went down and he wrote the check and gave it to me. One hundred dollars a month was a lot of money in that day, I'll tell you. When I reached home, I found it was for two hundred dollars. *He is going abroad,* I thought, *and has made it for two months this time.* But exactly one month later, another check for two hundred dollars came, and again the following month, two hundred dollars. But when he returned at the end of the summer, he continued to send two hundred dollars a month through the entire year.

I was learning to know Will Borden, one of whose characteristics was to always do better than he promised, more and not less than he led you to expect.

That fall we asked him to become one of the directors of the National Bible Institute, a school for lay evangelists we founded to train young men for evangelistic work in the city. We didn't ask him to join just to honor him—though he deserved it. We needed a man who could work and think and pray. We had frequent board meetings in New York, and he was required to come to every one of them—which he did. In fact, he spent a large portion of his summer vacation in 1911 on the hot streets of New York with us, taking a full share in meetings and other activities.

I find in my diary under the date of May 8, 1911, the following sentences: "Mr. William W. Borden came up from Princeton today to cooperate for a few weeks in the work of the National Bible Institute. A noble, generous, Christlike young man—a rare gift of God to the work under His care!"

We placed a desk for him in my office, and he continually showed an eager desire to enter into the work in every possible way. Responsibility for our four gospel halls was delegated to him, and he kept in close touch with the superintendents, counseling with them in regard to all the details. He investigated men who were being considered for positions of trust. He gave much thought and prayer to drafting the "Principles and Practice" of the National Bible Institute and prepared a document that has been of exceeding great value.

It's a joy for me to recall his first appearance at our Madison Square meeting in the open air. His address was brief, but remarkably vigorous and direct. He stood there as a witness to the saving power of Jesus Christ. As he spoke, I rejoiced that the large company of listeners had before them one of the manliest, purest, and noblest of our Lord's modern witnesses. His radiant face, unaffected manner, and joyous, fervent testimony to the power of the Christian faith made the occasion memorable.

As a member of the Board of Directors he was a valued counselor. He turned the white light of Scripture on every matter that came up for consideration. His presence in any meeting was a moral and spiritual tonic.

All his work began, continued, and ended in prayer. Again and again at our office he would suggest, before taking up the consideration of any important matter, that we should unite in waiting upon God. Prayer was to him the first means to be used in accomplishing any object. And how simple, direct, unselfish, and childlike his prayers were! He prayed as one confident that his heavenly Father would hear and answer.

To help us set our financial house in order, he brought in one of the women from the China Inland Mission's accounting department in Philadelphia to help us. She told us to never make a purchase, large or small, until there was money in hand to pay for it. She taught us to carefully estimate running expenses and put aside a daily proportion of our income, whatever it might be, to meet them. In this way there would always be funds in hand for coming charges.

"One cannot be running out every day to pay one's gas bill," she said. "But we can put aside a dollar and a half a day, or whatever the proportion may be, toward it. We do the same for our rent, fuel, electric light, taxes on property, and all other running expenses, so that the money is there when it is needed.

"We pay the rent on Saturday, for example, but on Monday we begin just the same putting away for the next month or quarter. And these funds are rarely drawn upon for any other purpose. We reckon that we have spent that money already. As to other things, we never give an order unless we have actual cash in hand to meet it. We do not draw upon probabilities."

And Bill added, "If the China Inland Mission can do it, never making an appeal for funds nor taking a collection, surely we can—by prayer and watchfulness! And I do think we ought not to buy even a broom until we have money in hand to pay for it."

We needed that advice because our work was growing fast and it was hard to keep pace with all it required. We needed permanent offices badly, places where students could meet for their classes, and a hall for the old Jerry McAuley Mission which had now passed into our care. And the neighborhood we hoped to locate in was a desperate one. On every corner in all directions you would find saloons or dance halls and a number of moving-picture houses. Thousands of young people thronged the streets every night, and there was no place open to them where the influences would be anything but harmful.

"We've got to do something now, Will," I said to him one day.

"What do you suggest, sir?"

"We need to gather a circle of praying friends, and then we need to map out this entire district. We need to know what is going on and what is available for us. We want to get into the thick of things."

So Bill set to work to make the needs and opportunities known and to gather friends together for prayer. We went out time after time to make a map showing exactly what was there and what was not. We found more than three hundred hell traps of various sorts all around us. We used this to let our friends know how to pray. Bill sent a circular out, signed with his own name, that included that map. We both felt that the National Bible Institute was to be a protest against iniquity and a ministry for reaching the sin sick and for protecting the innocent.

Bill's most important work that summer was in forming our Circle of Intercession. It was his belief that unless prayer kept pace with the building and planning and organizing, the activities would be in vain.

When he had to go back to school—his last year at Princeton—he agreed to come back for a series of seven weekly messages on the book of Galatians. I saw the long list of books he consulted as he prepared his talks. We marveled how he could be so thorough in his preparation for us and still carry his heavy courses in theology and ancient languages at the seminary. Our students really loved his class, and we always had between sixty and one hundred attending. His handling of this difficult epistle showed that he had completely mastered his material. His outlines were clear and comprehensive, and he made the book a living message to the hearers.

Early in 1912, we went through deep waters. We had to call a special meeting of the board—Bill came up from Princeton.

"We have done our best to keep clear of debt," I told the gathering, "but we have not been entirely successful. Despite our best efforts, we have incurred a deficit of five thousand dollars."

We passed that morning in earnest conference and prayer. We knew we would learn our lesson by the experience, but we had no idea how the deficit could be wiped out. We didn't want to appeal to our friends when we had made it a principle of the Institute that we would not do so. We knew, of course, that the Lord was able to provide, but we did not have a long period of time to watch and pray.

We adjourned for lunch and then came back in the early afternoon for re prayer and consultation.

At one point, Bill interrupted us.

"I must make the 2:04 train and shall have to run for it."

He was writing something as he spoke. He pushed it across the table to our treasurer, Mr. Hugh Monro, and then went out the door. It was a check for fifty-two hundred dollars! Without a word, he had paid the entire amount. Not one of us had dreamed he would do a thing like that. And before we realized it, he was gone.

But he gave us more than money. Late that spring, he finished his coursework and graduated from the seminary. His beloved mountains were calling him to Switzerland for rest and relaxation. In fact, his passage was already booked. He came by our office on his way to the boat and found that I was on the verge of collapse. My doctor had ordered me to take a complete rest and change, but there was no one to take my place at the office.

"Looks like I might have to change my plans a bit and help," he said. He ordered me on my way and said he would take over. He was sufficiently familiar with all we were doing, and it didn't take him long to be completely in charge. This meant he was not only responsible for the office and for the daily open-air meetings, the oversight of the students in their classes and their practical training, the charge of our four rescue missions and the monthly magazine, but also for the financial care of the entire operation.

Now I had no means to finance the work myself and had to depend on the Lord for all our needs. Bill carried this on, never becoming dependent on his own ability to meet our needs. He believed the promises of God were absolutely true and dependable, and he used this as an opportunity for proving the reality of his own faith and strengthening the faith of his fellow workers.

And the Lord put him to the test. Days passed without a dollar coming in. Our workers were dependent upon us for their salaries. He could have drawn on his own bank account to meet the needs, but he elected to spend the time in prayer alone and with friends, waiting on God for His gracious answer. And the answers came, and with them such a sense of the reality and nearness of the living God that none of us ever forgot it.

That was the hottest summer in New York in years. Bill's mother had moved to the city with him. He was also caring for an invalid uncle and frequently went to the shore to minister to relatives he had there.

He prepared an article for our magazine that summer that was prompted by a remark Dwight L. Moody had made: "The world has yet to see what God can do with a man who is fully consecrated to Him." Bill's highest ambition was to be just such a man, and he was learning how high a price he had to pay. He learned that it all came down to one word—obedience. He knew the source of power was the Holy Spirit "whom God hath given *to them that obey him*" (Acts 5:32 italics added).

This is the article he wrote:

> There must be a definite determination to do God's will—a will to obey. Christ laid down the conditions of discipleship as denying self and following Him, and that is just what is required here. Each one must examine his life and put away all sin, not holding on to anything which the Spirit tells him he should let go.
>
> One of the hardest things anyone can have to do is to confess he has wronged another. But we read, "If thou bring thy gift to the altar, and there rememberest that thy brother hath aught against thee, leave there thy gift before the altar, and go thy way; first be reconciled to thy brother, and then come and offer

thy gift" (Matthew 5:23-24) . . .

Questions of life work also need to be met squarely and the enquiry honestly made: "Lord, what wilt Thou have me to do?" The answer may not come at once, but there should be a willingness and determination to do His will, whatever service it may involve, at home or abroad . . . Ask yourself, Have I ever fully surrendered? Have I definitely consecrated myself, put myself at God's disposal, to use as He deems best?

It must be admitted, however, that there are those who at some time of vision or conflict have won a victory and taken this great step, and yet have not subsequently had real power in their lives . . . Cases differ, but may we not say that it was probably through failure to make this principle of complete obedience permanent in their lives? Christ's rule for discipleshsip as given in Matthew 16:24 has been referred to above. Do you know how it reads in Luke, and what the additional feature is which has there been preserved for us? It is just one word: "If any man would come after me, let him deny himself and take up his cross *daily* and follow me." Daily—that is the thing to note . . .

The need for daily application of this principle appears in two ways: first, old questions which have been faced and downed as we thought, will come up again; and secondly, there will arise new problems which were not covered by the original act of consecration. Many who have faced the question of life work and decided for the foreign field illustrate this. It was at tremendous cost they made the decision, and possibly there was the thought that afterwards all would be plain sailing. But no: the same old problems had to be fought out, and there were new ones too to face. The principle of Christ's supremacy could not be lost sight of for a moment. Satan, when defeated, left Christ but for a little season. How much less, when he has been ousted from our lives at some conference or on some mountaintop will he despair of finding a foothold when we are on the plane of everyday living again. Obedience, which is the price of power, must not only be absolute but daily. Are we paying this part of the price? . . .

Mr. Speer in his *Principles of Jesus* has indicated four great guiding principles that our Lord laid down—namely purity, honesty, unselfishness and love. These are simple and plain enough; yet how many of us are checking up our every thought and word and deed by these? . . . Our personal habits, our amusements, all our intercourse with others, business or social, should be considered in this light. We must seek not merely to avoid quenching the Spirit; we must be careful lest we grieve Him.

Obedience, absolute and unqualified, which is made a daily principle of living, carried even into little things, this is the price of power . . .

How the power will manifest itself in our lives need not concern us here. The saying still holds good—"The world has yet to see what God can do with a fully consecrated man." Only as filled with His Spirit can we hope to win men from darkness to light and to faith in Christ.

Shall we not each one resolve, from henceforth, to obey Him absolutely in all things, small and great?

Before I got back to the office, Bill was put to the test of being obedient to responsibility no matter what the cost. Duty must come before pleasure.

His class at Yale was having its first reunion. He was able to get away for the weekend, but he had to be back on the following Monday. That meant he had to miss the climax of the proceedings—the Triennial Banquet. His classmates were shocked that he would think a board meeting of the Institute more important than that illustrious affair—they did their best to dissuade him from returning.

One of them, his former roommate Mac Vilas, said later, "We might as well have talked to the Rock of Gibraltar."

He was able, though, to return to New Haven on Tuesday in time for the class picture, the parade to the football field, and the game in which Yale beat Harvard 9-6.

Once I was finally able to return to the office, Bill and his mother sailed for Switzerland. You would have thought he would take the time to fully relax, but he had another important task.

He was on the board of Moody Bible Institute of Chicago and on a committee the president, Dr. James M. Gray, had appointed to prepare a statement setting forth the doctrinal standards of the institution. He had already prepared such a statement as part of his application to the China Inland Mission, and he had a copy of our statement from National Bible Institute covering the same ground—a document he had also had a significant part in preparing.

You'd think his work was never done.

Dr. James M. Gray

(President, Moody Bible Institute)

It was with great pleasure that the Board of Trustees of the Moody Bible Institute appointed Mr. William Borden to the position of director. And he responded by informing us of his own pleasure in accepting. He was also pleased to accept the responsibility of serving on a trustee committee charged with drafting a doctrinal statement for the Institute.

Mr. Borden took this assignment seriously. Following his graduation from Princeton Seminary, he wrote me the following letter. He was traveling to Switzerland on the steamer *Kronprinz Wilhelm* at the time. He dated the letter July 21, 1912:

> Dear Dr. Gray—In accordance with your wishes I am taking this opportunity to draw up my suggestions for the proposed doctrinal basis of the Moody Institute.
>
> *First, the purpose:*
>
> As I understand it, the need is for a statement embodying what we feel is essential to sound doctrine in the teaching and work of the Institute. This statement should be an aid to the trustees, not only as a standard for checking up the teaching staff, but also to guide them in the selection of new trustees at any time—written assent to the doctrinal basis being required of all present and future members of the Board of Trustees as well as the teaching staff, and also a pledge to give notice of any future change of opinion, and willingness to resign if requested to do so.
>
> *Second:*
>
> What is the essential to sound doctrine? I feel that the inspiration and authority of Scripture; God: His being and attributes; Christ: His person (Deity) and work (atonement); the Holy Spirit: His person and work; man's sinful state and need of regeneration; the way of salvation from the guilt of sin (justification by faith alone) and from the power of sin (sanctification); the return of Christ and future rewards and punishments are the essentials.

Third:

The order and phrasing of the statement. I would say at once that I do not feel that it will be possible to employ Scripture language only, both from the nature and extent of the ground to be covered and the exigencies of the present day with its requirement of great exactness. We should, however, seek to be as brief as may be consistent with clearness. Coming then to the actual phrasing, I would suggest the following:

DOCTRINAL BASIS
OF
THE MOODY BIBLE INSTITUTE

We believe in the inspiration, integrity, and authority of the Bible. By this is meant a miraculous guiding work of the Holy Spirit in their original writing, extending to all parts of the Scriptures equally, applying even to the choice of words. Moreover, it is our conviction that God has exercised such singular care and providence through the ages in preserving the written word, that the Scriptures as we now have them are in every essential particular as originally given, so that the result is the very word of God, the only infallible rule of faith and practice, containing all things necessary to salvation and sound doctrine.

We believe that there is one living and true God, a spirit infinite, eternal and incomparable, etc. (see Westminster Shorter Catechism). And we believe that in unity of this Godhead there are three persons, the Father, the Son and the Holy Spirit (see Episcopalian Prayer Book).

We believe in the deity of our Lord Jesus Christ and in His death on the cross as a true substitute, and that His death was a sufficient expiation for the guilt of all men.

We believe in the Holy Spirit as a Divine person, distinct from the Father and the Son, who convicts the world of sin, regenerates and dwells in the true believer, quickening and empowering him in all his life and service.

We believe that all men are by nature sinful and unable to save themselves, and that "except a man be born again, he cannot see the kingdom of God."

We believe that men are justified by faith (in Jesus Christ) alone and are accounted righteous before God only on the merit of our Lord and Savior Jesus Christ.

We believe that sanctification is a work of God's free grace whereby, being renewed in the whole man, we are enabled more and more to die unto sin and to live unto righteousness.

We believe in the second coming of our Lord, as a personal, visible and glorious advent on this earth.

We believe in the everlasting conscious blessedness of the saved and in the everlasting conscious punishment of the lost.

As a conclusion I would suggest an adaptation of the paragraph in the Moody Church statement to the effect that while specifying these doctrines, we by no means undervalue or set aside any Scriptures of the Old or New Testaments.

Of course I do not pretend that this is final, but it embodies my thoughts for the present. I hope you can read it all. Kindly keep the enclosed typewritten statement with this letter (of which I have no copy by the way) as I would like to refer to the two together in Chicago when we meet next fall, D.V.

Sincerely yours,
WILLIAM W. BORDEN

10

Mrs. Howard Taylor

(Daughter-in-law of J. Hudson Taylor)

The very day that Borden took his last examination at Princeton also found him in New York with Dr. John R. Mott, deep in plans for the work he was to take up in the fall in connection with the Student Volunteer Movement.* A three months' schedule had been made out for visits to many colleges. He was to speak especially on the need in the Moslem world, before sailing for Egypt on his way to China. It was felt that a few months at Cairo, in the language school, would be of advantage, not only for the study of Arabic and the Koran, but of Islam in general, before attempting to meet it in the strongholds of Western China.

Released from his responsibilities in Mr. Shelton's office, Borden spent a few weeks in Switzerland, climbing the Jungfrau and the Wetterhorn, and returned to New York refreshed for his work in the colleges. Then came his ordination, which took place in the Moody Church, Chicago, as its elders recorded:

*The material in this chapter has been adapted from *William Borden,* by Mrs. Howard Taylor, pp. 195-201.

> He was one of our boys. This was the church of his childhood . . . Here he returned for ordination after completing his Seminary course, and as we examined him in view of that step his testimony rang true as steel to every cardinal doctrine of Holy Writ.
>
> On September 9, 1912, we set him apart to the ministry of our Lord and Saviour Jesus Christ in a foreign land, little thinking that his ministry was to be to our Lord Himself in the better land.

The service was simple but impressive, marked by contrasts that gave the daily papers a good deal to say at the time. That a man of his age and prospects should turn away from all the world could offer and devote himself to a life of loneliness and hardship in a remote province in China, "the darkest and meanest section of the Orient," as one paper seriously said, became a nine days' wonder. But another Chicago daily gave an account of the proceedings that must have arrested attention, printing in full on its front page the hymn that seemed to summarize all there was to be said:

> When I survey the wondrous cross
> On which the Prince of Glory died,
> My richest gain I count but loss
> And pour contempt on all my pride.
>
> Were the whole realm of nature mine,
> That were an offering far too small;
> Love so amazing, so divine,
> Demands my life, my soul, my all.

Borden did not see the papers. That side of the matter was painful to him. In a circular letter to twelve Princeton classmates who kept up correspondence, he mentioned the fact of his ordination, adding: "I am sorry there was such unnecessary publicity, and hope you fellows will discount what was said very liberally."

The real impressiveness of the service lay in the love and sympathy of the great assembly for one who had grown up among them, whose consecration to Christ they knew full well. This was illustrated in the sermon by Dr. James Gray, dean of the Bible Institute; the charge given by Dr. John Timothy Stone, pastor of the Fourth Presbyterian Church; and in the prayers with which Borden was committed to the Lord. From the very spot Moody had so often preached, the ministers and elders gathered round Bill. One later said, "We set him apart for the work to which he was called. The hands of the lowly were laid upon his head. The Holy Spirit filled him. The grace of the Omnipotent was in his life."

That grace was very real in his mother's experience as well—in the hour which was to her the climax of her sacrifice. From his childhood she had consecrated him to the Lord, and his call to missionary work had come as an answer to her many prayers. Yet, since his father's death, she had learned to lean upon him in everything, and the very thought of separation seemed at times unbearable. Firm as a rock, there had been no wavering in his purpose. He knew as well as she did that her deepest desire was one with his own. They stood together, and his strength had helped her no less than his tenderness. But the separation had hitherto been prospective—now it was coming near. His ordination meant, as Mrs. Borden realized, that they were committed to the sacrifice that seemed as if it must cost her her very life.

And then—there is no explaining it apart from

the presence of the Lord Himself—as in that hour she held back nothing, a wonderful peace filled her heart. Physical weakness, even, was replaced by strength, so that she was able to meet all the demands of the dreaded situation when it came, with gladness. For there is a fellowship with Christ which infinitely compensates any cost at which it is won.

To a friend who expressed surprise, about this time, that he was "throwing himself away as a missionary," Borden replied: "*You* have not seen heathenism."

He had seen it, and the constraining love of Christ made him, as one of his Princeton classmates put it, "a missionary, first, last and all the time." Yet, to him, souls were just as precious in America as across the ocean, and his responsibility as great for all whom he could reach. One of his friends wrote later about him, "Most of us look for occasions which may afford a suitable opportunity for soul-winnning, and excuse our lack of devotion and diligence because we feel that such an opportunity is not present. We continually hesitate to broach the subject of another's salvation, lest the occasion should not be favorable. Yet Borden found such opportunities continually."

Visiting with his mother, for example, in the home of some relatives, he became concerned about the butler, who was giving way to drink. At dinner one evening, when not sober, he let some ice cream slip off a plate, nearly ruining an expensive gown. Learning that he had been dismissed, Mrs. Borden mentioned the matter to William. It was not their responsibility maybe, but the following Sunday his mother's maid, walking in the direction of the butler's house, heard quick steps behind her and found William at her side.

"Melanie," he said, "I am going to inquire about our friend. Couldn't we have prayer together that God will speak to him today?"

They stopped right there on the street, then Borden went on to the house. The butler truly turned to the Lord that day. Only two weeks later, he took pneumonia and died.

Do you think Bill Borden ever regretted the effort he had made to go see him?

Fennell P. Turner

As General Secretary of the Student Volunteer Movement, I was not only able to help organize and direct his speaking tour but also to monitor its progress and effect.

Bill's message in the colleges was of the sort to appeal to a strong personality. As a lad, he had seen the heathen firsthand. Fuller knowledge had since deepened his conviction that the two hundred million in the Moslem world were the hardest as well as the most neglected field for missionary enterprise. Those very difficulties attracted him.

He would speak of Kansu—that lonely, far-off province in northwest China with its three million Moslems among a hardy population of Mongols, Tibetans, and Chinese. That was the sphere in which he hoped to labor.

Peking was much more central, even more strategic. There were more than a few mosques in the capital. He might have been able to have a post as organizing secretary for work among Moslems throughout China, but he was looking for a harder job. Because Kansu was isolated, thrust out between Mongolia and Tibet, because the missionaries were few and the work difficult, because the people he longed to reach were there in multitudes and no one was set apart for work among them, that was the place of his choice.

He would speak of Ho-chow with its bigoted, proud race of Moslems—Arabs by descent. There, too, were the Tung-hsiang, remnants of the old Hun tribes in the mountains, long since converted to Islam at the point of the sword. And there were the Salas from distant Samarkand with their Turkish speech and faces, Moslem exiles who had tramped across Central Asia hundreds of years ago to find a home beside the Yellow River. And the virile, dominating sons of Islam were mingled in the western part of the province with Tibetans from the border marches and Mongols from north of the Great Wall. Further, the Great Road running through the province—itself a thousand miles from east to west—led on across the Gobi Desert to the Moslem heart of Central Asia, linking city after city in which no missionary had ever labored. But the road also gave access to the mingled peoples of that vast region—one of the most neglected fields in the world. That waiting heart of Asia—how it appealed to him, because so few were willing to lay down their lives that those people, too, might hear the message of redeeming love.

He spoke of the brave men and women who were

there, representing the two missions working in the province. He told about George Hunter and P. C. Mather of the China Inland Mission who were a forty days' journey westward from Kansu—almost as far as the nearest missionaries on the other side. More than sixty cities in Kansu itself were without a witness for Christ. Eighty percent of its population were still unreached—three million Moslems for whom no one could be spared because the inadequate staff was absorbed in work among the Chinese. There was no doctor or hospital in the entire province.

That was the picture he painted. With such a background he was able to bring a sense of reality to the missionary work he represented. The joy and inspiration of a great task possessed him, and he could not speak of missionary work, even in its hardest phases, as sacrifice. To him it was privilege of the highest order.

I noticed that he took two books with him wherever he went. He used them in his talks. One was Dr. Samuel Zwemer's *Unoccupied Mission Fields of Africa and Asia.* Its facts gave him strong arguments to use in the preaching of missions.

The second book, a little paper-covered volume, he read and reread and marked all the way through. It was called *The Threefold Secret of the Spirit* by James H. McConkey, and was divided into three parts. The first dealt with the secret of the incoming of the Holy Spirit. The second covered the secret of His fullness. And the last presented the secret of His constant manifestation in our lives. One sentence Bill marked heavily was, "The supreme human condition of the fullness of the Spirit is a life wholly surrendered to God to do His will."

Life for Bill was not a question of being or having this or that. It was simply a question of the will of God—knowing it, doing it, loving it. And such a life, he knew, was possible only through the indwelling of the Holy Spirit. This colored his messages and gave them gladness and power.

Bill began his tour at Schenectady, New York, in September and visited thirty colleges and seminaries before sailing for Egypt in December. He would spend one to three days in each place and have interviews and meetings with the students. He would often open an interview with the question, "Are you steering or drifting?" The inquiry would open up the subject of a student's choices in life. Everyone knew how easy it was to drift. If a man said he was steering, then Bill would say, "What is your goal and who is with you on board?"

The uttermost for the utmost was the price as he saw it—the uttermost of surrender on our part for the utmost of what God will do in and through us. It was a high ideal. Often Borden would meet one to whom that question seemed too deep with a different challenge: "Are you willing to be made willing?"

Some students wondered if people would think Bill's directness of appeal might seem to lack sympathy with the other person's point of view. But they agreed that it was the sort of thing that drew out the best in a man and would make it obvious if a person were willing to do God's will. One thing that was obvious to everyone was that the speaker had himself counted the cost—his sailing date was already set.

He would say that he wasn't pleading the cause of missions. "The case is there. All we ask is a verdict. If ten men are carrying a log, nine of them on the little end and one at the heavy end and you want to help, on which end will you lift?"

He looked on difficulties as merely a challenge to faith and consecration. He didn't minimize the difficulties, but he did emphasize our Lord's own words, "The things that are impossible with men are possible with God."

Those were fruitful months. William was used to leading students in many colleges and universities to give their lives to foreign missionary service. The last letter I received from him enclosed the "declaration card" of a Student Volunteer who had signed it after Bill's visit and had then sent it to him in Cairo. In years to come there will be missionaries in many fields who owe their decision, under God, to William's unselfish service during his last months in this country.

A Yale Classmate

Bill came to the seminary where I was a student in November of the year he was touring colleges for the Student Volunteer Mission. He came to my room one afternoon and lay on my couch. He'd caught a feverish cold and needed to rest.

I couldn't let the opportunity go by without talking, of course, and in a joking way I asked him when he was going to marry.

He replied seriously that he thought it was cruel for a man who was going into one of the most difficult of missionary fields to ask any girl to go with him, because the woman always fared the worst—often succumbing when the man survived. He said he had no intention of marrying—it would hinder his highest efficiency in the field he had in view.

I know he strongly approved the rule of the mission with regard to outgoing missionaries, whether men or women, remaining unmarried for the first two years in China. He knew the rule would allow him to give undivided attention to the study of the language and would enable him to become adjusted to the people.

And I'm sure he had counted the cost of what it would mean after those two years were up—and many years later—when he would still be living in "one of the most difficult of missionary fields."

In one of his books he had marked this poem:

> Yes, without cheer of sister or of daughter,
> Yes, without stay of father or of son,
> Lone on the land and homeless on the water
> Pass I in patience till the work be done.

Mrs. Borden

(His mother)

It was just like William to want to leave at once, as soon as his tour of colleges was finished. I'd had such a difficult time getting him to come spend his twenty-fifth birthday with me on November 1. And our friends who were leaders of the Volunteer Movement certainly didn't want him to leave so soon either. He had had such a strong, effective work among the students. They urged him to give them more time.

His work with the students ended on December 10, and it would have seemed so natural for him to have stayed through Christmas and the holidays. He could have left in early January. But the SS *Mauretania* was sailing on the seventeenth and would reach Port Said on New Year's Day.

"I know it will give me only one week for packing and final preparations, Mother," he said, "but I'll have two or three weeks longer in Cairo on the other end."

Time for William was one of his most important stewardships. I could not hold him back. He was ready to go, and I had to let him.

He kept up his visits to the Yale Hope Mission right up to the end. He had placed it in the care of Mr. Don O. Shelton of the National Bible Institute. His love for that place was just the same as when he had helped start it six years before. I remember how he had gone into it with all the hopes and fears of a beginner. He loved the new director, Bill Ellis—the two of them were a wonderful combination when they were together in the meetings.

Dr. Henry Frost told me that he asked a much-traveled visitor from abroad what had impressed him most since coming to America.

He said without hesitation, "The sight of that young millionaire kneeling with his arm around a bum in the Yale Hope Mission."

William spent his last Sunday quietly with me. We went to church in the morning, not even imagining it was for the last time. And on the following day he took part in a meeting we held regularly in our home to pray for the Moslem world. Dr. and Mrs.

Frost and Mr. Shelton came to dinner that night. William was leaving the next day. We wanted five or six of the men with whom he had been most closely associated in work for God to gather with us for a last hour of prayer and fellowship.

They prayed that their beloved friend might be kept in safety throughout his long journey, that he would be guided and upheld in all his ways. And then William prayed for us and for the work that each one represented. He was so strong and vigorous in body and mind that night. We were all so sure he would have a long and useful ministry. But in less than four months—happily none of us knew it then.

But in the quiet of my room that night, worn and weary and sad, I fell asleep asking myself again and again, "Is it, after all, worth while?"

And in the morning, as I awoke to consciousness, a still small voice was speaking in my heart, answering the question with these words: "*God* so loved the world that *He* gave *His* only begotten Son—"

It was strength for the day—and for all the days to come.

Each day, from his childhood, William and I had prayed that the will of God might be done in his life. And as we parted on the *Mauretania*, we prayed again. I wonder if it occurred to him later, as it did to me, that we had prayed that he might be taken to China and made a blessing among its millions of Moslems—but only, "if it be Thy will"?

The next day I sent him a Christmas letter written on the back of a faded sheet bearing a Christmas carol that had as its chorus: "Glory in the highest and goodwill to men, Peace on earth, peace on earth."

I wrote beneath the verses and on the back of the page:

> Darling, a blessed Christmas to you! This is one of the old song-sheets used at "89" (our home), years and years ago, when we were all together. Never did I realize so clearly the missionary meaning of Luke 2:10 ("Good tidings of great joy which shall be *to all people*") as I did yesterday morning while sitting by your side in church.
>
> Just one word more: I will never cease to be grateful for the rich blessing you have been to me, Dear, a comfort and strength all your years to your devoted mother. What a rich New Year is unfolding before you! It was so beautiful having you with us in our little prayer circle—just one more of the loving touches God has put to these last days.

11

Hugh Munroe

As treasurer of the National Bible Institute, I was fully aware of what Mr. Borden was doing financially to help with the Lord's work. Therefore, the news following the probate of his will was no surprise to me. He had made it out in the fall of 1912, and it went through probate a few days after his sailing for Egypt.

It struck many of us as very interesting that the will of J. Pierpont Morgan was read about the same time. That man died, possessed of nearly one hundred million dollars. Bill Borden had one million. Though Morgan was a devout believer, as indicated by the preface to his will, "I commit my soul into the hands of my Saviour, in full confidence that having redeemed it and washed it in His most precious blood, He will present it faultless before the throne of my Heavenly Father," he at seventy-five years of age left only little more than half of what Bill left at twenty-five.

Mrs. Borden told me that when she and her sister went through William's checkbooks they found that during the three years he attended Princeton Seminary he gave about seventy thousand dollars to

Christian work. This surprised them because he had never mentioned to anyone that he was giving. He seems to have been a person who studied the need and then gave so he could help. Few Christians of ample means succeed in realizing such a degree of detachment from their possessions to the point of removing all sense of restraint in their dealings with their fellows of every station. Borden had learned the art of administering wealth on a large and generous scale without complete self-effacement.

His Yale friend Charlie Campbell recalls that Bill always followed the injunction, "Let not thy left hand know what thy right hand doeth."

Charlie said, "He insisted that not even his initials should appear when a list of benefactions was published. It almost seemed to irritate him if he was found out. His best friends never knew even a small percentage of the gifts he was making. I bet many surprising incidents would come to light if all who had been helped by him could be induced to tell their stories. Bill's checkbooks show how little he spent for himself and how much he was doing for others."

One of Bill's Princeton classmates said, "I've been told that he felt one of his temptations was to own a car. He never purchased one because he thought that for him it would be an unjustifiable luxury.

"I remember one Saturday afternoon in New York going with him to the auto show in a hall at Madison Square Garden. He knew all the various makes and pointed out to me the advantages of the different cars. But we left the hall to take dinner at the YMCA and spend the evening down at the Katherine Slip and Doyer Street Missions. And he had filled his pockets and mine with copies of St.

John's Gospel to use in personal work."

His mother said, "I think William's real reason for the stand he took about a car was that he deprecated the luxury seen in the lives of so many Christians. He didn't feel justified in using his money, which he held distinctly as a stewardship, for any such purpose. All the time we were in Princeton, I think he was longing to get away into simpler living."

The news of his gifts touched and startled people all across the world. Think how much he gave, when in 1912 one could buy a loaf of bread for five cents and a fine house for three thousand dollars.

Friends at Moody Church in Chicago said no other giver gave more to their Fresh Air Work, to their Sunday school, and to the general expenses of the church than Bill during the last years of his life. He left the church one hundred thousand dollars so that it could take advantage of its downtown setting to preach the gospel to a teeming city of thirty different nationalities.

He divided his inheritance, bequeathing practically all of it and giving one fourth for use in Chicago, another quarter in other parts of the homeland, the third portion for work in China, and the remainder for work in other foreign countries.

He left one hundred thousand dollars to the National Bible Institute and the Moody Bible Institute as well. He gave fifty thousand dollars each to Princeton Theological Seminary, the Board of Foreign Missions of the Presbyterian Church, USA, the Board of Foreign Missions of the Presbyterian Church, US (South), the Board of Foreign Missions of the United Presbyterian Church, and to the Chicago Hebrew Mission. He gave twenty-five thousand dollars each to the Nile Mission Press, the

American Bible Society, the Chicago Tract Society, and the Africa Inland Mission. Of what was left, the China Inland Mission and the three Presbyterian boards were made the residuary legatees.

He insisted that his money be used only in support of those men who held absolutely to the deity of Christ and His vicarious atoning death for sinners.

"It is further my desire," so says the will, "that the said bequests hereinbefore made be used and disposed of in accordance with the following recommendations by me, to wit: That each of said bequests be used for and in connection with missionaries and teachers who are sound in the faith, believing in such fundamentals as the doctrine of the divine inspiration and authority of the Scriptures, the doctrine of the Trinity, including the deity of Jesus Christ, and in the doctrine of the atonement through the substitutionary death of our Lord Jesus Christ."

His friend, Dr. John R. Mott, said he had seldom met a person who showed such penetration of mind in estimating the worthiness of causes toward which he would give. He didn't want to make just good use of his money, but the best use. "One was conscious of the fact that he regarded himself as a trustee and in no sense a proprietor. His thoroughness in investigating objects was nothing less than remarkable."

Mott felt that these traits, together with Bill's prayerfulness in determining what to do with his money, marked him out as a model to the young men of his generation to whom God may have entrusted financial power.

A friend who knew him in Chicago wrote:

This was Borden: quiet but powerful; saying little but doing much; rich but self-denying; humble in spirit but imperial in purpose; a general in organization, but always willing to be a private in service. He declined our urgent invitation to preach in the Moody Church on the ground that he was not capable, but he was not ashamed to tell of his faith in Jesus on the street corner. His heart went out to the uncared-for, Christless millions of Kansu; but he did not overlook the worthy widow, orphan and cripple in the back streets of Chicago, as some of us well knew. He was intent upon seeking to win for Christ and His service the young men of our colleges and universities, and to this end the last months of his life in America were given; but that did not prevent his thinking of, praying for and giving to the care of little children and the aged.

Dr. Henry Frost said in connection with this, "We seldom thought of it while he was with us. But I refer to his bequest of $250,000 to the mission that I may mention his desire with regard to a portion of it. He asked that a hundred thousand dollars might be invested in order that the interest upon it should be used for aged and infirm missionaries. A young man of twenty-four thinking of and providing for old and infirm missionaries! Could anything be more far-reaching in thought and sympathy?"

12

Mrs. Howard Taylor

Cairo, with its brilliant sunshine and lure of color and all its dust and heat, was not new to Borden. He had visited it with the Reverend Walter Erdman eight years previously, when they traveled up the Nile to Aswan, seven hundred miles toward the heart of the dark continent. The colossal ruins of Karnak, the rock-hewn tombs of the kings, the temples of Thebes and Philae, the statues of Memnon, and other remains of the ancient world stirred them profoundly. From Aswan William had written:

> Upper Egypt completely fulfills my expectations—the Nile itself, the contrast of the fresh green fields with the quivering sand beyond, the groves of date palms, villages of flat-roofed houses, camels with their dusky riders crossing the desert which stretches away as far as eye can see. It really is delightful.
>
> Our first donkey ride in Egypt took us through the town and out into the desert to the Bishareen encampment. These people are Soudanese, I believe, and very different from any others we have seen. They wear their hair hanging in loose gimlet-curls, about eight inches long. They are quite black and

have clear-cut features, at least those we have seen have.

But now it was as a missionary, not a traveler, that Borden was in Cairo—that great city that Dr. Maltbie Babcock wrote of as "a huge melange, an ecumenical potpourri, a huddle of the ends of the earth and the first and last of civilizations."

It was not at Shepherd's Hotel, where he had stayed before, but at the YMCA that he took up his quarters. Met at the railway station by Dr. Zwemer, he was soon introduced to the very heart of things in the missionary community. He found himself unexpectedly in touch with China as well, for a missionary from Hong Kong had discovered a Chinese student at the El Azhar university, of whom he spoke to Borden on the day of his arrival. The lonely student was from Kansu, the very province in which William was hoping to labor. The man was so cut off from his own country that he did not even know of the fall of the Manchu dynasty and the establishment of the new republic. Borden was eager to meet him, as one of his early journal entries records:

> January 7, 1913
>
> Went to El Azhar with Mr. Gairdner. Met the only Chinese student there—the first Chinese Moslem I have ever seen so far as I know.

What a world of interest El Azhar proved to be, with its thousands of white-turbaned students from many lands including Russia, Persia, North and Central Africa, Abyssinia, India, and Arabia. There were also about two hundred professors, or Sheikhs, every one of whom had spent at least twelve years studying at the university. Old as it was, dating from the tenth century and entrenched in Moslem bigotry and pride, it was not unaffected by the Christian influences at work around it. Only a few months before Borden's coming, an article had appeared in a religious paper in which one of its professors had written:

> Do not say that it is impossible to convert an Azhar Sheikh and bring him to Christ, for with God all things are possible. Was I not a fanatical sheikh in El Azhar, and was I not by God's grace converted? Today I pray that my fellow-sheikhs may be won even as I was.

Many students were attending the Monday evening meetings for Mohammedans that winter, at which Michael Mansour was speaking with great power. "Mighty in the Scriptures and in the Koran as well," he was attracting great crowds. A foreign missionary was always in the chair to keep order and Borden was soon in his element distributing Arabic Scriptures and tracts.

From the YMCA headquarters it was no great distance to the American Mission where Dr. Zwemer lived and where the Monday evening meetings were held or to the compound of the Church Missionary Society at which a good deal of Borden's time was spent. For it was there that the students of the new study center took their courses in Arabic with the Reverend W. H. T. Gairdner and in Islam and practical work with other missionaries. Eight or ten were taking the complete course and were attending Dr. Zwemer's lectures at the YMCA and the theological seminary. It was a keen, lively circle, and one to which Borden was soon contributing a good deal. Mr. Gairdner found him "brim full of energy and hope, bringing a new element into our midst."

Dr. Samuel Zwemer

(Missionary to Moslem world)

I never saw a man come to Egypt with eyes more open to see the kingdom of God. Other men come to see the dead Pharaohs, to study history, or to join the great company of tourists all over the land, never once lifting their eyes to see the fields "white unto harvest." Borden had not been in Cairo two weeks before he organized the students of the theological seminary to attempt a house-to-house canvass with Christian literature for the *entire* city with its eight hundred thousand people.

Here was a man with the frame of an athlete, the mind of a scholar, the grasp of a theologian regarding God's truth, and the heart of a little child. He was a man full of faith and love—so tender in the relations of home life that our children used to nestle upon his knee as if they had known him for years. Yet he was a comparative stranger to them.

Knowing that he had to learn Chinese, he came to Cairo to perfect himself in Arabic. Some people shrink from the foreign field, questioning, "How could I ever learn the language?" Here was a man who deliberately set before himself the task of learning not one but two of the most difficult languages in the world, before entering upon his ministry.

At Yale, at Princeton, in Cairo we see him digging deep, thinking deep, and studying hard. He did not import doubts to the Orient, he imported his great convictions of the eternal truth of God. When he lived in Cairo, he was a friend to the Coptic Christians and the Armenian Christians. He was a brother to the American missionaries and to the British missionaries. He attended the Scotch church and the American church, and at the last all sorts of Christians met together to do him honor.

Bill Borden's Letters from Cairo

JANUARY 15, 1913

Saturday we had a very interesting session at the student Center and in the afternoon I went out with Mr. Gairdner to visit old Cairo and the Church Mission Society hospital. As this is well on the outskirts of the city, we got a good ride on our wheels. Later we called on a Syrian family in which Mr. Gairdner thought I might be received as a paying guest. They had a surprisingly nice place, and as it was an unexpected visit the cleanliness and order could not have been put on for our benefit. They insisted upon giving us refreshments, which consisted of some kind of liquid in little liqueur glasses, quite harmless, followed by a teaspoonful of grated cocoanut put into our mouths by our hostess!

Sunday, I started my first work for Mohammedans by distributing *khutbas,* little sermons in Koranic style gotten out by the Nile Press. It required some courage to take the first plunge, with my two words of the spoken language, "Do you read Arabic?" and begin offering these booklets on the streets. But I soon found that it went very well, and I have given out about fifty already. Only one or two have declined to take them.

Monday night I went to my first service in Arabic. It was at the American Mission headquarters and most interesting. A few weeks ago, it seems, a rumor got abroad that Mudbuli, a Moslem saint, had come out of his tomb and had taken refuge in the Greek church near by—a pretty good exchange, considering the dilapidated state of the tomb. Of course, the more educated scoffed at the idea, but multitudes believed it, with the result that there was quite a riot at the time.

Soon after, in a newly published Moslem book attacking Christianity the author said that the resurrection of Christ was just like this Mudbuli affair, the story of a lot of silly women. He called attention to this as a great joke! But there is a Moslem convert here, Michael Mansour, a former El Azhar student, who went to the place where the book was printed and got out five hundred circulars saying he would answer the above statement, debating it with anyone who would come.

This was the gathering Dr. Zwemer and I attended. He was half expecting a riot, as the place was packed with Mohammedans. The meeting opened and closed with prayer, however, and Mansour spoke for nearly an hour, holding their attention so that there was no disturbance and only one or two went out. It was a great triumph, and though I could only understand an occasional word, I was very glad to be there.

This afternoon I had a fine time, going on into the native bazaar with Dr. Zwemer to a book shop. It was near the Azhar, and we had a fine chance to get rid of all the *khutbas* we had, to students and others, and one of them bought a Gospel. Among the books we purchased were some Korans; and when these were put in the bottom of the carriage, there were strong objections immediately and they had to be put up on the seat beside the driver.

The outing was great fun, for we not only did this work but had a great time together. This bookshop man, by the way, is an enquirer who has been already a couple of times to see Dr. Zwemer. Things are on the jump here, especially when you are with Dr. Zwemer.

February 5, 1913

Yesterday, we had a report of our *khutba* distribution and found that all had gone off without excitement, save in the case of Dr. Zwemer and the students who had accompanied him to a fanatical part of the city. With them, too, all went well for a time, till they met an old man who wanted to know by whom the tracts had been written and who got quite excited when he learned that it was a former El Azhar student who had become a Christian.

Dr. Zwemer, seeing that there was going to be trouble, tried to get the students away and to disperse the crowd by going into a shop. But the crowd waited outside, and there was no way of escape. Finally, with the old man continuing his attack, they were all marched off to the police station.

The officer looked at the *khutbas* and listened to the charge.

"Why," he said, "this is nothing but Christianity! You can read about this any day." And he let them go.

The result was that the wind was quite taken out of the old man's sails, and they were able to distribute a lot of *khutbas* right in the police headquarters which would have been inaccessible to them otherwise. They invited the people to come to the Monday night meeting for Mohammedans, and the man who made the trouble was there all right last Monday night. Sorry I missed the excitement! But I have another section of the city which is less liable to afford interest of this kind.

FEBRUARY 12, 1913

Dr. Zwemer has just started a new thing—putting Christian notices into the daily papers, inviting inquiry by letter or in person. He has already received several answers.

My Arabic is going rather slowly just at present. I seem to have struck a snag. It certainly is difficult! However, I hope to overcome by the help of God and with due perseverence . . . Dr. Zwemer preached a fine sermon at the American Mission, Sunday night. Afterwards we met an American girl, a graduate of Holyoke, whom we had both known in Student Volunteer days. She had just arrived with a party. It was nice to see someone like that.

FEBRUARY 17, 1913

I have bought a "tarboush," as they call the red fez here, to wear when we go to investigate Islam in some form or other, that I may not be so liable to be the one investigated. It is really remarkable how effective such a slight change proves as a disguise. A great many of the natives wear European dress, you see, save for just this hat. So when we put it on they do not know whether we are "Christians" or not, and can be quite sure that we are not tourists. All of which is valuable.

I bought mine as we were going to a *zikr* the other night with Mr. Swan of the Egypt General Mission, but it rained so that we called it off . . . I have not yet explained what a *zikr* is: briefly, a repetition of the Moslem creed by Dervishes, until they are exhausted. Tomorrow is the Prophet's birthday, so we expect to see plenty of them as they go on all night.

We are still distributing *khutbas*, and it is going all right. Dr. Zwemer seems to think that as they are read more and more by Mohammedans all over the city there may be some kind of an outburst that would hinder our distributing them freely. We shall soon have the Sermon on the Mount, however, ready for distribution in the same form, and that no one can take exception to.

FEBRUARY 20, 1913

I mentioned in a recent letter that we were going to see some *zikrs* at the celebration of the Prophet's birthday. This we did on Monday night, and it certainly was interesting, though I fear I shall not be able to describe it at all adequately.

A large piece of level ground had been taken and tents erected in a great square, an entrance being left at one side. Each of the tents was assigned to a Dervish order, or some department of the Government. The tents themselves were very attractive, made of Oriental tapestries in rich red hues, and lighted with glass chandeliers, each of which had a dozen or more big candles. The effect was very brilliant. The floor in the center of each tent was occupied by the Dervishes, who stood or sat in a circle, or if there were many of them in two long rows facing one another.

They all repeat more or less the same things—the name of Allah, the Moslem Creed, the opening sura of the Koran, or the ninety-nine beautiful names of God—but the accompanying motions differ. Some sit and move their heads, first to one side, then to the other and down on the chest, swaying their bodies at the same time, back and forth. Others stand, bending from the waist in rhythmic motions. This was what the Merganiyeh Order were doing as they repeated:

> La illaha il Allah,
> Muhammed rasul Allah.

At first they would bend slowly, then gradually increase the pace till they were all going full speed, the leader keeping time by clapping his hands or coming in with a solo refrain in the marvellous way of intoning these fellows have. One could not watch them without feeling the grip of the thing, although knowing it was nothing but a deliberate attempt to induce a state of ecstasy or auto-hypnosis. The Government has put a stop to many of the worst excesses, so that now these big functions are comparatively tame and they seldom go to the former extremes.

One man Mr. Swan pointed out to us is known as "the Protestant Dervish." He preached repentance from sin, very much like a Protestant minister, though, of course, without any mention of Christ as the atonement and the One who delivers from the power of sin. He had quite an audience, which he managed much as an evangelist would at home—getting responses from them and letting them ask questions, first of all telling them good stories to get them in a favorable humor. Dr. Zwemer calls him "The Billy Sunday of Islam"!

The next night, Tuesday, was the climax of the celebrations . . . The Dervishes all paraded through the city, chanting and dancing, each Order making a company with its Sheikh riding on horseback. I followed them a long way and saw them as they came into the grounds at Abbasiyeh. It was really very picturesque.

In the evening there was an immense crowd, chiefly to see the fireworks—"an invention of the evil one" that Mohammed certainly never supposed would come to be connected with his birthday. The crowds hurrying through the streets, the brilliant lights and all the excitement, reminded me very much of the festival of Juggernaut in Madras.

MARCH 1, 1913

Thursday night we had an interesting trip with Mr. Swan into the back streets of Cairo. The *zikr* we were going to see had been changed, we found, to another night, but just before reaching the place we came into a cemetery and heard the chanting of another *zikr* coming from a little old house off to one side. The star-lit night, the graves and their surroundings, all made a wonderful setting for the weird intonation we could hear so distinctly, even at a distance.

Mr. Swan talked with the men at the place we went to, telling them of Him who is *the* Way. The same Arabic word is used in the Bible for "way" as these Dervishes apply to themselves, in the sense of sect or order. It was really quite remarkable how they listened and seemed to take it all in.

At one place, while I was waiting for the others, I was asked by a woman to read an Arabic letter for her. I was wearing the fez, of course. And later in the evening when we met a drunken Moslem who was rather talkative, he addressed me as "Mahmoud Effendi"—Mahmoud being a Moslem name!

MARCH 1913

Dear Dr. Frost:

An event here in Cairo has saddened us all and made me realize afresh the heroism of the doctor in his every-day work. I refer to the sudden death of Dr. M. Pain of the Church Missionary Society, a man beloved by hundreds and filled with the Spirit of Christ. I only met him twice, soon after my arrival, and the next thing I knew he was dead.

I wish I could give you the full medical particulars, as you would be interested. As far as I could ascertain he was attending a patient suffering from spinal meningitis. The patient coughed in his face, and infection followed apparently. This took place on a Sunday, and the following Wednesday, about 5 A.M., he passed to the home above.

His funeral, attended as it was by a great crowd of natives and Europeans, was a most eloquent testimony to his loving faithfulness in serving his Master . . .

I remarked to a friend as we left the cemetery, "Now we must work all the harder, for the time is short."

Straub, A Young German Missionary

His zeal made me ashamed of myself. He always had his pockets full of *khutbas* and lost no opportunity to distribute them. He was greatly interested in getting acquainted with the national life and the doings of the Dervishes. For this purpose we went to Mohammedan festivals where *zikrs* were taking place, each wearing a red fez so as not to attract attention.

The last time we worked together was on the Thursday during Passion Week, just before he fell so critically ill. It was the anniversary of the saint Abul Ela in Bulak. What crowds of people were there to be seen—people of all classes and ages, men and women, people who were well and people who were sick. As these occasions partake of the character of national holidays, all sorts of amusements were going on. The illumination was truly amazing.

Our chief interest was in the various *zikrs* and we were drawn to one tent from which the sound of chanting reached us—"Allah, Allah!" For a long time we stood, side by side, watching the strange motions of the men who were swinging forward and backward in strict rhythm, shouting. The tempo of these motions grew quickly and steadily; "Allah, Allah" became hoarser and hoarser, until finally nothing but heavy breathing could be heard. Several of the Dervishes fell unconscious to the ground. We noticed one man close beside us wrought up to the highest pitch and saw foam gushing from his mouth. We, too, felt the excitement and were full of pity for these poor, deluded people whose way of worship was so unworthy.

About midnight we started, arm in arm, for home and had scarcely seated ourselves in the trolley when Mr. Borden took his remaining *khutbas* and handed them to those nearest to him.

Gamil B. Hassoon

It was a real pleasure and honor to have Mr. William Borden live in my house in Cairo. He was perfectly at home with the poverty my family lived in.

It is beyond power to describe his great zeal and diligence in studying the difficult Arabic language. But though he was so absorbed, so fond, so overwhelmed with his studies, he did not make Arabic his only aim. He looked to what was higher and nobler and appointed a large portion of his time for reading the sacred Scriptures. His Bibles—and he had many of them—were all visited by his eyes. There were many remarks on their margins made in his handwriting and many underlined texts, which showed that he had chosen them and probably put them into memory. His reading the Scriptures was not a daily duty. He read them because he loved them.

His life and deeds agreed to what he read. He loved everybody, and as a rule when you find one who loves like that you may be sure of his love to God. In a conversation I had with him I found that he loved the YMCA with a wonderful love. When our talk turned on the Arabic branch, his love to it seemed not less than to the other. I knew that he wanted to strengthen the Arabic branch by all the means he could—financially, morally, and mentally—so that it might attain a level with the greatest European associations and even surpass them if possible. Many times he expressed to me his pleasure in the progress this branch had taken in the short time since it was organized, despite all obstacles.

His love to the Orient and Orientals was a profound, true love. He was very pleased with many of our noble customs which he had not experienced before. He was very kindly sociable in our society—and in a few days, not exceeding the number of fingers of one hand, he became one of us—Orientalist, with the full meaning of the word. He loved to communicate and mix up himself with us and we with him, preferring to change his long-accustomed habits and acquire our ways, so that he might prepare himself with what would agree with the taste of Orientals among whom he hoped to live. The kindness and sociability God endowed him with were very great.

He denied himself and had a special motto written on a paper in his pocket: "My Lord, enable me to conquer my will and overcome my desires." And he had another motto: "*Not my will but Thine* be done."

We had talked about this, and I shared my problems with controlling my thoughts. He wrote me a note which I have kept:

> I can sympathize with you in the matter of controlling your thoughts, for that is a thing we all have to fight for. You are right in saying we may commit great sins in our minds, though we do not do so outwardly. This is the view of sin which Christ gives us in the Sermon on the Mount, Matthew 5 and 6. However, I believe that in this as in all other things we can gain the victory by faith, through His aid, who was "tempted in all points like as we are, yet without sin." . . .
>
> The principle on which we want to work is to crowd out the bad with the good. If we merely seek to put away evil without replacing it with active good, we may find that worse things come in. I have been helped by the suggestion that when we are tempted to harbor evil thoughts, we should at once think of Christ or repeat some verse of Scripture—and in this way spoiling the picture, so to speak, by letting in a flood of light. Our object must be to bring "every thought into subjection to the obedience of Christ" (2 Corinthians 10:5).

What impressed me most was his strong faith. He did not think that there was anything impossible to do in the service of the Lord. In the books he and I read, we found that it is nearly impossible to enter into Tibet or Afghanistan to bring the gospel to the Mohammedans there. But that fact was not to shake his faith. And he went further, believing that it was most possible that the gospel should in a few years be preached in Mecca, the center of Islam itself. He loved to be where the fight was hottest. The unoccupied fields of the Moslem world were his target, and all the time he was preparing himself for the evangelization of such fields.

He was very fond of Mohammedans. Once he came home with a very pleased face.

"What is it makes you look so happy?" I asked.

He had met, he said, two Azhar Sheikhs and stopped them by the way. They spoke to him in Arabic, something he could not understand. But he did all he could and led them a long distance to Dr. Zwemer's house. Showing them the house, he said, *"Koll yom gomaa,"* meaning, "every Friday." And he spent with them fifteen minutes by the roadside, using the few Arabic words he knew.

I asked him to repeat the Arabic he used, and we had great fun of it! But it was good enough to make those men understand that he wanted to gain them for Christ, and they parted with peace. To my full belief they went to Dr. Zwemer's on Friday.

William had a winning look and an attractive spirit. He was meek and kind. My love to him is very great, and I remember every movement of his. Although he was a rich man, he denied himself the privileges of rich people and lived as simply as any missionary could. He was following the footsteps of Jesus.

Once a friend said to me, "Your guest is a millionaire."

"I do not know anything about his dollars," I replied.

When I came in, I told Mr. Borden what I heard, but he did not confirm it.

"People often mistake us," he said, "for the rich condensed milk firm that bears the name Borden."

This put me into an opinion that he was not so rich, and I kept on treating him as a brother, not as to please a millionaire. I am sure he liked it that way.

13

Mrs. Samuel Zwemer

My husband had just left on an evangelistic trip to Jedda, only thirty miles from Mecca, when I received a telephone call from Mr. Hassoon. It was Good Friday, March 21. He told me that William was far from well.

I went over at once to their house and found Will in bed. He had been to see the doctor already and had been ordered to get complete rest. He had a headache and some fever, but nothing serious apparently. He'd been out a good deal in connection with his canvass of the city, and we thought that perhaps he had caught a light case of influenza.

When I called the next morning, I learned he was better. But we were all surprised to hear later in the day that he had been taken to the hospital. The doctors thought it might be heat stroke, but they were not allowing anyone to see the patient.

Easter Sunday came with its wonderful opportunities to witness to the people of the resurrected Lord, but all of us felt a little apprehensive. The more so when one of our band went out to the hospital that afternoon to enquire about Will. He was told that Mr. Borden had cerebral meningitis!

We were all stunned. I chased the doctor from place to place and finally saw him personally that evening. He would not give any hope, only that Will was no worse and that serum had been injected into his spinal cord.

We cabled home at once. But we could not reach Mrs. Borden. She had already left by steamer with her daughter Joyce to join William in the Lebanon mountains for the summer. She was sailing for Alexandria direct, but they were not due in Gibraltar until April 1, and we could not reach them by telegram for some reason.

Fortunately, we were able to reach his sister Mary who had just returned from India with her family and was still in London. On hearing of Will's sickness, she set out for Cairo at once, but could not arrive until April 2.

Daily we sent cables back to his home, for one day he would seem so much better but the next be so much worse. We knew that a great volume of prayer without ceasing was going up to God for this young man.

We all knew the risk of infection was very great, but we could not keep away. I was able to visit and pray with him regularly—I had to have fresh news to send to his home. Mr. Gairdner visited him daily too, and Mr. Giffen of the American Mission was allowed to see him once and again.

We knew Will's suffering was intense. He was fighting the bravest battle of his life, and there was no shrinking back now. He told me that from his childhood he had prayed with his mother that God's will would be done in his life.

Of course, all of us were thinking of our young doctor missionary who had suddenly been called

Home so recently. Will himself had stood beside his grave.

I recall the words of Adam McCall, one of the first missionary pioneers in the Congo and one who, too, had fallen:

> Thou knowest the circumstances, Lord. Do as Thou pleasest, I have nothing to say. I am not dissatisfied that Thou are about to take me away. Why should I be? I gave myself, body, mind and spirit to Thee—consecrated my whole life and being to Thy service. And now, if it please Thee to take me instead of the work I would have done for Thee, what is that to me? Thy will be done.

Miss Whiting

(Mrs. Borden's sister)

Someone had to be available to answer the telephone and keep in touch with William's large circle of inquiring friends. Since my sister had left on the boat, I set aside everything to be in the Borden home in New York. Everyone, it seemed, wanted to know the latest news.

I telephoned Mr. Frost, and he came up of his own accord and remained until the following day at noon. He was most kind and could do a good deal of inquiring, writing notes, and so on, while I had to be out. Mr. Delavan Pierson suggested a circle of prayer in which he and his wife would join, so Mr. Frost arranged it with Mr. Don O. Shelton.

Mr. Shelton telephoned me that hardly anything else had been thought of that day—all the workers of the Institute met with him in the morning and the board of directors in the afternoon. He said that prayer would continue strong and steady until William's recovery was assured.

We sent word to Dr. A. B. Simpson and telephoned the Erdmans of the seminary. We telegraphed people around the world, trying not to leave out anyone my sister would have wanted to know. We sent word to his friends at Moody Church. Charlie Campbell spent all one afternoon with me. In many ways he made William seem so near!

I found it a real blessing and joy to be at my sister's home at such a time. So many friends called with words of love and admiration and sorrow. Even the men were not ashamed of their tears. No one, *no* one could understand why it had happened. Dr. Erdman said, "It is the strangest, most mysterious working of the divine providence I have ever experienced. The world has such need of William!"

Gamil B. Hassoon

As soon as I stepped into the room, he, in spite of his great suffering, gave me a wonderful smile which is printed on my memory. He then sat up in bed, but very soon had to lay himself down again.

I sat by his bedside for a short time and spoke to him with all the oriental and brotherly kindness I could master at that critical moment. I was greatly astonished that all his sufferings did not hinder him from showing gratitude and love.

I passed my hand over his forehead and wiped away the drops of sweat that stood there and asked God to help and cure him. He smiled again and held my hand in his and pressed it very gently and warmly in such a manner which made me feel his love.

He was not so very able to speak much, but his eyes spoke and transmitted to my heart all that was in his heart and mind.

And thus I left him for the last time.

Dr. Samuel Zwemer

I had just returned from Jedda and was in quarantine at Suez when I received the terrible tidings of Borden's illness. I went to him at once and found that the doctors were hoping that his splendid physical constitution would be strong enough to hold out through his illness.

He recognized his sister Mary who had just come from London. She pitched right in and helped the nurses do all that their love and skill could devise. She told him that their mother was coming soon.

She told me that he would speak in his semi-consciousness, often saying, "Poor Mother! Poor Mother!" He would speak, too, about his work in his delirium. It was much upon his heart.

On the fifteenth day, he was slightly better although in the morning the doctor had no hope. My wife had done heroic work, both in visiting and in praying and in keeping in touch with Mrs. Borden by cable.

On the eighteenth day, I left for Port Said to meet the steamer. It had hardly cast anchor when I got aboard at 5:00 A.M. and was able to bring them the news that he was still living. You can imagine how relieved they were.

Ada von Fallenberg

We could hardly sleep that last night before we got into Port Said. I had lived with the Bordens for some years as companion to Joyce, so I was with them on this trip.

Dr. Zwemer's news calmed our hearts at once, but we knew time was of the essence and left at once for Cairo.

We went ashore in small boats, and everything was very interesting and strange. Our steamer was overrun with Arabs and Negroes of all descriptions. The harbor sparkled with light and bright colors. The ride from the water's edge to the railway station was also fascinating, with the first high palms, the veiled women, and the bright picturesque costumes of the Arabs.

We left by train at 8:00 A.M. and had a fine run to Ismailia, following for many miles the banks of the Suez Canal. It was surprising to find the canal so narrow and that the largest ocean steamers could yet pass through.

Almost at once after leaving the canal, the desert began—long stretches of sand with beautiful vistas, far away, where the sand appeared bright pink.

Here and there would be a green patch, wherever water was to be found, although near by the same soil was just barren wilderness.

After a long time the Nile deposit began to appear—dark soil, very different from the sandy stretches, and getting more and more black as we came into the cultivated land of Goshen. There, Arab life was all around us. Already in the desert we had seen camels wandering about, either alone or with bedouin in floating garments. Now we passed native villages—mud huts, veiled Moslem women, men loading camels, families riding on donkeys.

We had morning prayers and sang hymns. I especially remember the one with the chorus: "Stayed upon Jehovah, hearts are fully blest; Finding as He promised, perfect peace and rest."

This meant so much to Mrs. Borden and Joyce.

At Ismailia, half-way to Cairo, a telegram was brought to us: "William not so well." Dr. Zwemer said it had been like that all the time. Having reached a certain satisfactory level, his condition then worsened every second day, improving again the next.

We went on. It was only a few stations farther that a second telegram came to Dr. Zwemer, directly to the car.

It was the end.

I cannot describe that next hour on the train. Dr. Zwemer was the greatest comfort—but, oh, it was dreadful! It broke my heart to see Mrs. Borden and sweet little Joyce. We reached Cairo at 1:00 P.M. William had passed away at 9:00 A.M. I cannot believe it even yet—

The funeral had to be the same afternoon. His death was absolutely peaceful, without any struggle; he just simply stopped breathing. Dear, dear Mrs. Borden—what sorrow, what loss!

Mrs. Borden

I do not want you to think of us as overwhelmed, for we are not. God's loving care and mercy have been evident on every side, and it has been a real joy to be in the place where William, in those few short weeks, became so honored and loved—and was so *happy!*

The missionaries have all been most kind and thoughtful, and Dr. and Mrs. Zwemer wonderful in their loving sympathy and untiring efforts on our behalf. Dr. Zwemer has been son and brother in one. He loved my son and could scarcely speak of him with unbroken voice. Mr. Gairdner, head of the language school where William was studying, visited him daily through all his illness, though it is considered dangerous to go near the sufferer. The nurses, they tell me, were devoted. And so were the Arab boy attendants, night and day, keeping the flies away. As yet, it is all more like a dream than reality.

But I wanted to tell you just one thing that you may not hear from anyone else: when we saw him, it seemed as though William had been transformed into the very likeness of Christ, through suffering. I should never have known him, his beard and moustache had grown, and the contour of his face was changed.

We had been in doubt as to whether to go to the hospital to see him, altered as he would inevitably be, but thank God, we did. We were told not to go near the bed, to stay at a safe distance. We approached a long, low building, standing right on the ground—it seemed as though we might be going to the tomb itself. The question, "Who will roll us away the stone?" was on my lips. The door was opened, and immediately we were in the presence of all that remained here of our William.

I was so shocked at the change that I turned to beg Joyce not to look or to come in, but she had already done so, and said in the gentlest voice, "But Mother, did you see how he looks like all the pictures of Christ—the crucified Christ?"

I looked again, and then indeed I saw.

One hardly dared speak of it to others, fearing it would be thought irreverent or fanciful. But I did mention it to Douglas in Mr. Gairdner's hearing, who quietly said, "Yes, and you only stood at the threshhold. If you had gone nearer you would have seen the resemblance more clearly."

I said that, standing there, I could only think of the words: "His visage was more marred than any man's."

"Yes," Mr. Gairdner said, "*His* visage—more marred than any man's."

It put such a holy touch upon it all.

"Perfect through suffering." It was as though we had been permitted a glimpse into the mystery of suffering, human and divine, and had seen that through it God had, so to speak, given the final touches to William's life.

Two verses say it all: "Christ Jesus my Lord—for

whom I have suffered the loss of all things, and do count them but refuse, that I may win Christ, and be found in Him."

And: "Jesus, looking upon him, loved him."

14

Mrs. Howard Taylor

A friend who was with Mrs. Borden wrote:

> The funeral was very informal. The Anglo-American hospital is beautifully located on the island of Gezira in the midst of green meadows, palms and roses. From there we went to the American cemetery. How strange it was to have Arabs doing everything! A great many friends and missionaries were present, the Syrian gentleman, too, in whose family William had lived. They are lovely people, simply devoted to William. Mrs. Zwemer says that the conditions in their home were perfectly all right, and that there was no risk to health in being there. The food was good, and William was in no way tired or run-down when he contracted the disease.
>
> Mr. Gairdner read the service and the Scriptures. Dear old Dr. Watson prayed, and so did Dr. Giffen and Dr. Zwemer. We sang "Face to face with Christ, my Savior." I shall never forget it as long as I live. We stayed to the very last. The sun was going down, and the glow in the west was wonderful. They planted flowers on the grave, and it looked very beautiful.

A missionary who was present added:

As we sang hymns during the service, the Mohammedan grave-diggers, standing a little way back, looked astonished, for it was all in such sharp contrast with the hideous and meaningless wailing which takes place at a Moslem funeral. Still greater was their astonishment as they watched the little company of native Christians weeping over the grave of a foreigner—one they had learned to love as a brother. Never shall I forget the feeling that came to us with our closing hymn:

Sing it softly through the gloom,
  While the heart for mercy craves;
Sing in triumph o'er the tomb—
  Jesus saves, Jesus saves!

Our very souls were lifted out of their mourning into a glad and glorious triumph, and we could indeed say: "O death, where is thy sting; O grave, where is thy victory?"

Even the crude, varnished coffin could bring no pang to the mother's heart, different as it was from the casket that would have been provided at home. As she saw it lowered into the grave, containing all that was mortal of her son, a feeling, not of pain at the outward sorrow that swept over her, but of wonderful joy and comfort in the thought of that entire life spent for Christ—scarcely a moment of it wasted.

The words of Dr. Zwemer linger longest, spoken in the place and among the friends Borden had last loved. There in the American Mission were gathered representatives of all forms of Christian service through the city and with them men wearing the fez and the white turban of the Azhar student. Few leaders had influenced Borden more than Dr.

Zwemer, and none could have had truer insight as he spoke at that Memorial Service from the words: "I have fought a good fight, I have finished my course, I have kept the faith" (2 Timothy 4:7-8).

Dr. Samuel Zwemer

One of the great characteristics of this life we mourn and in which we rejoice is that our friend and brother was a soldier every inch—a soldier of Jesus Christ. Those who knew him best knew that he was fighting, and now he "has fought."

He won that greatest victory of all, the victory over himself. Charles Kingsley, who knew that life was not a bed of ease nor a garden of roses, wrote:

> The very air teems thick with leagued fiends;
> Each word we speak has infinite effects;
> Each soul we pass must go to heaven or hell . . .
> Be earnest, earnest, earnest . . .
> Do what thou doest as if the stake were heaven
> And this thy last deed ere the judgment day.

And Borden *was* earnest. No one could say of him that he trifled with the thing men are trifling with all around, the great talent of life.

He won the victory over his environment. By some the victory has to be won over poverty; by others over heredity, or over shame and temptation. But Borden won the victory over an environment of wealth. He felt that life consisted not in "the abundance of things a man possesseth," but in the abundance of things which possess the man.

He won the victory in great measure over sin and temptation. There is not a young man living in America today who has not to fight a deadly battle for character. Borden fought and won—for two reasons: he always carried his sword and always looked up for strength. He was a man of the Bible, as his Greek Testament and the Bibles he used for study and devotion show, and he was a man of prayer. Even in the smallest details of life, he looked up for wisdom and strength.

Another great thing that comes into a man's life is "urgency." At college, as well as here in Cairo, Borden felt the call of urgency, and to him this was linked with thoughts of the Moslem world. I found underlined in his Testament: "I must work the works of him that sent me while it is day."

The real secret of this full-orbed life was that, like Paul, Borden could say, "I have kept the faith." How many men in these days—men at the beginning of their ministry, or in pulpits, or at the end of their service—have to cry, "God knows, I have lost the faith." Borden held to the Bible. He believed it from cover to cover. His faith had been tested, for he had met destructive criticism in his college course. He had a grasp of the oracles of God, and to us it was a great joy to see that *belief in the Book* had made him a missionary.

He gripped the essentials, he had no shibboleth, his was no narrow creed. This gathering is indicative of his wide fellowship. His Egyptian brethren could never have told to which regiment he belonged in the army of God. He was too big a man to wear the distinctive colors of any regiment. He kept the faith—but he did not keep the faith to himself.

Ask the man who met him.

"Henceforth there is laid up for me a crown of righteousness." He now wears the crown of life and glory. "O God, to us may grace be given to follow in his train!"

Only today, I was reading in *Pilgrim's Progress* of the death of Valiant for Truth:

> "My sword I give to him that shall succeed me in my pilgrimage, and my courage and strength to him that can get it. My marks and scars I carry with me, to be a witness for me that I have fought His battles who will now be my rewarder." . . . So he passed over, and all the trumpets sounded for him on the other side.

* * *

I heard Him call
  "Come follow," that was all.
My gold grew dim. My soul
  went after Him.
I rose and followed. That
  was all.
Who would not follow if they
  heard Him call?

(Author Unknown)

Moody Press, a ministry of the Moody Bible Institute, is designed for education, evangelization, and edification. If we may assist you in knowing more about Christ and the Christian life, please write us without obligation: Moody Press, c/o MLM, Chicago, Illinois 60610